The Best of ZZ TOP®
FOR BASS GUITAR

Y0-CFT-442

Transcribed by: Steve Gorenberg
Editors: Carol Cuellar and Aaron Stang
Cover Design: Robert Ramsay and Ken Rehm

"ZZ TOP" ® and the "ZZ TOP" ® logo are registered trademarks.
All rights reserved. Unauthorized duplication is a violation of applicable laws.

Warning: Any duplication, adaptation or arrangement of the compositions contained in
this collection, without the written consent of the owner is a infringement of U.S.
copyright law and subject to the penalties and liabilities provided therein.

CHEAP SUNGLASSES ... 8
GIMME ALL YOUR LOVIN' ... 14
GIVE IT UP ... 24
GOT ME UNDER PRESSURE ... 28
I'M BAD, I'M NATIONWIDE ... 19
LA GRANGE ... 34
LEGS ... 3
ROUGH BOY ... 36
SHARP DRESSED MAN ... 42
SLEEPING BAG ... 39
STAGES ... 46
TUBE SNAKE BOOGIE ... 51
TUSH ... 56
TV DINNERS ... 59
VIVA! LAS VEGAS ... 64

Guitar Solo:

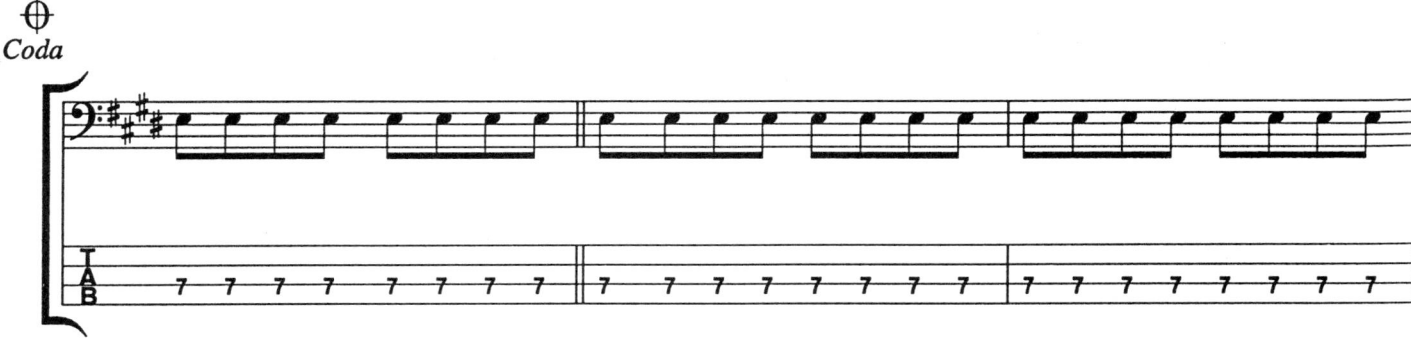

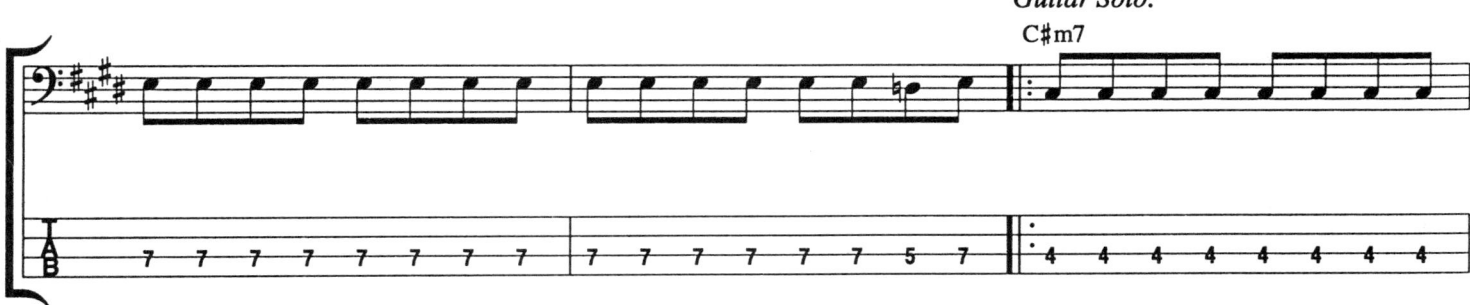

Verse 2:
She's got hair down to her fanny.
She's kinda jet set. Try undo her panties.
Every time she's dancin', she knows what to do.
Everybody wants to see, see if she can use it.
She's so fine, she's all mine.
Girl, you got it right.

Verse 3:
She's got legs, she knows how to use them.
She never begs, and knows how to choose them.
She got a dime, all of the time.
Stays out at night, movin' through time.
Oh, I want her. Sure I got to have her.
The girl is alright.

CHEAP SUNGLASSES

Words and Music by
BILLY GIBBONS, DUSTY HILL
and FRANK BEARD

Cheap Sunglasses – 6 – 1
P0986BGX

Copyright © 1979, 1992 HAMSTEIN MUSIC COMPANY (ASCAP)
International Copyright Secured   Made In U.S.A.   All Rights Reserved   Used by Permission

10

Interlude:

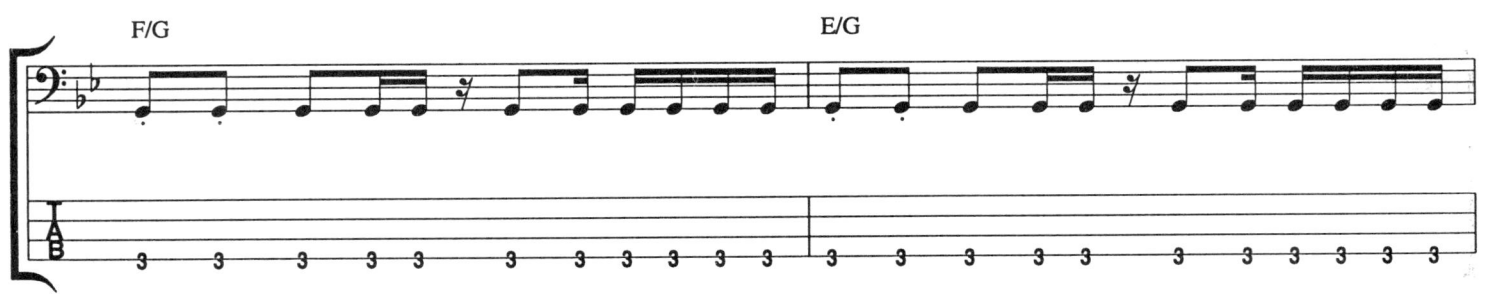

Guitar Solo:

Cheap Sunglasses – 6 – 3
P0986BGX

11

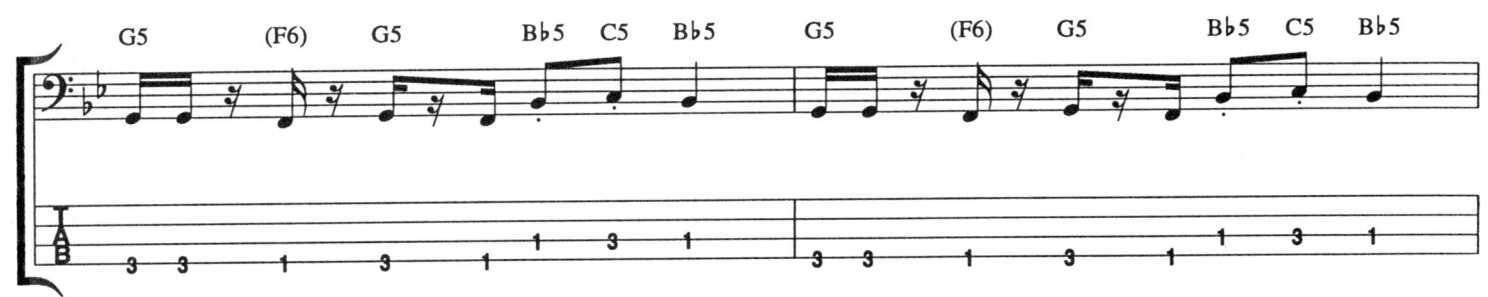

Cheap Sunglasses – 6 – 4
P0986BGX

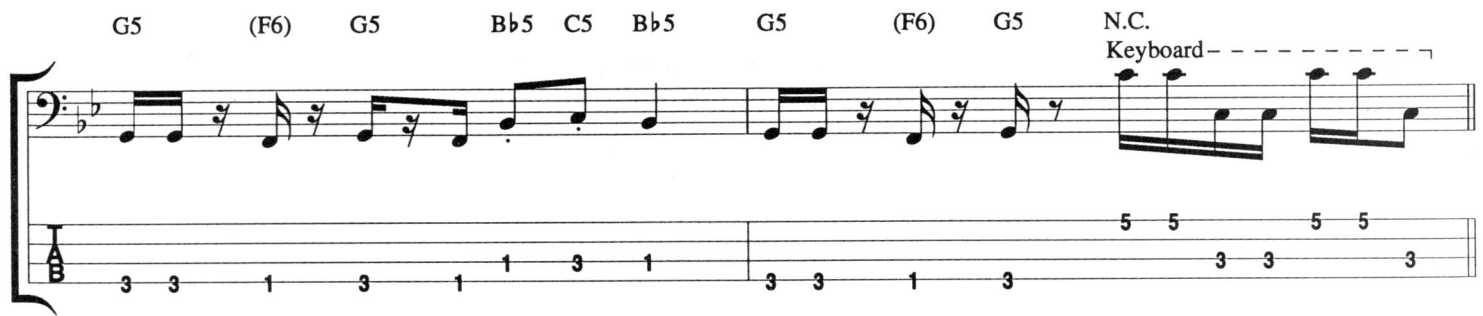
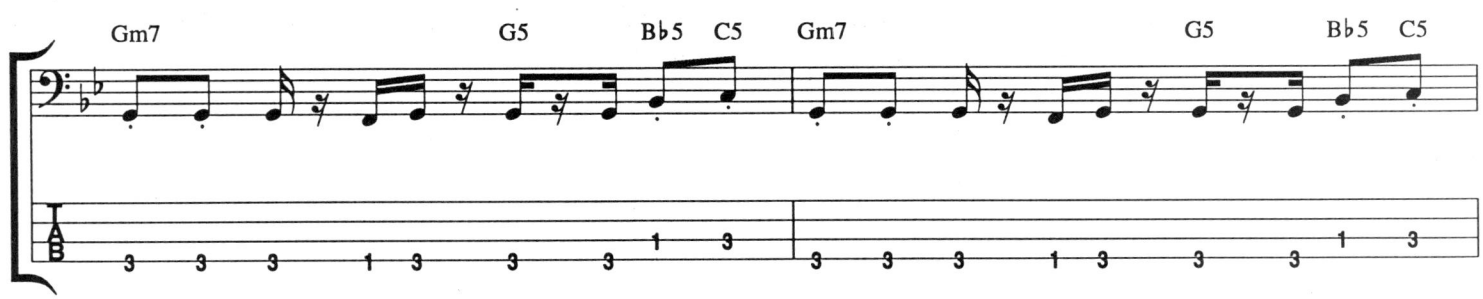
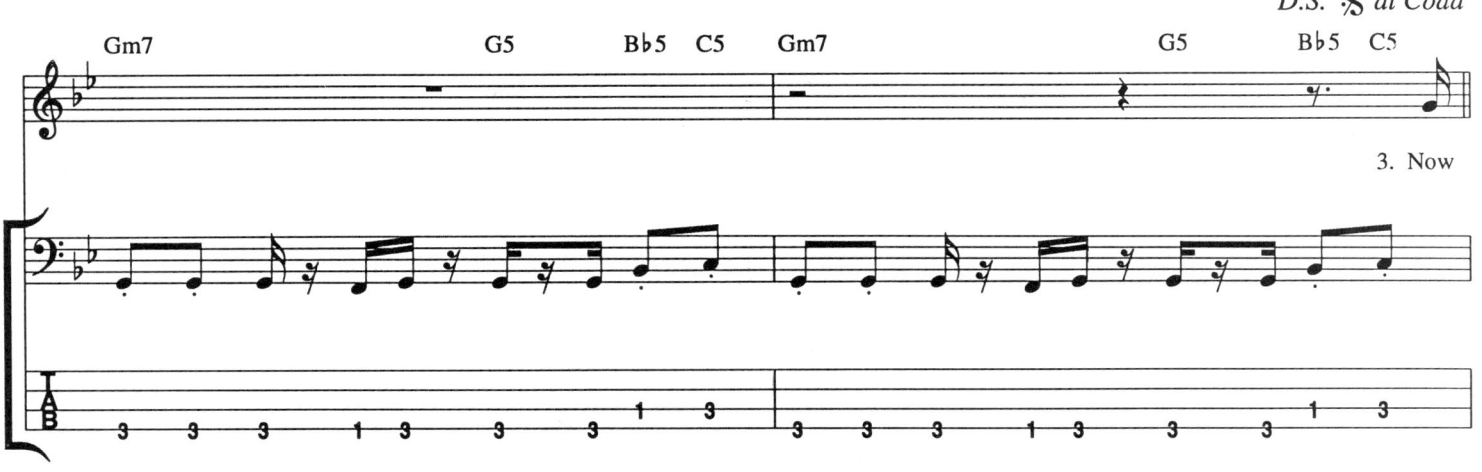

Cheap Sunglasses - 6 - 5
P0986BGX

poco ritard   dim. poco a poco

Verse 2:
Spied a little thing
And I followed her all night.
In a funky fine Levis
And her sweater's kinda tight.
She had a West Coast strut
That was sweet as molasses.
But what really knocked me out
Was her cheap sunglasses.
Oh yeah, oh yeah, oh yeah.
(To Interlude:)

Verse 3:
Now go out and get yourself
Some thick black frames.
With the glass so dark
They won't even know your name.
And the choice is up to you
'Cause they come in two classes:
Rhinestone shades
Or cheap sunglasses.
Oh yeah, oh yeah, oh yeah.
(To Coda)

Cheap Sunglasses – 6 – 6
P0986BGX

GIMME ALL YOUR LOVIN'

Words and Music by
BILLY GIBBONS, DUSTY HILL
and FRANK BEARD

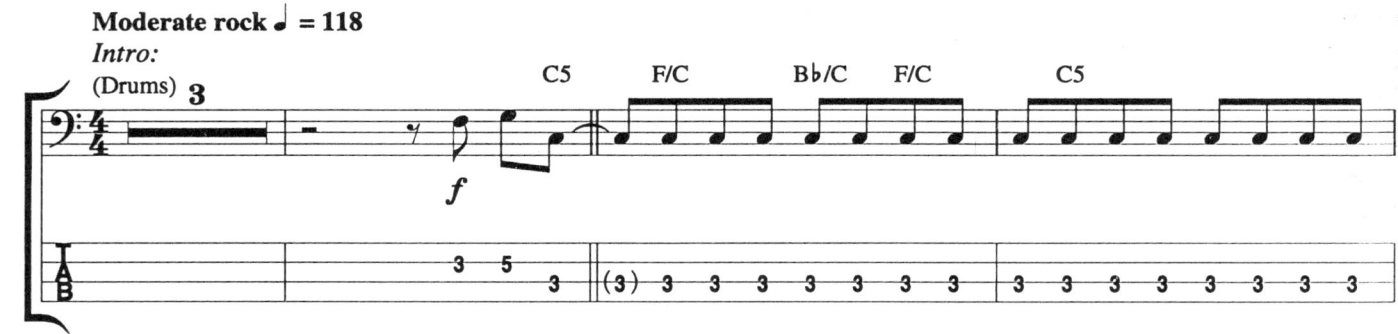
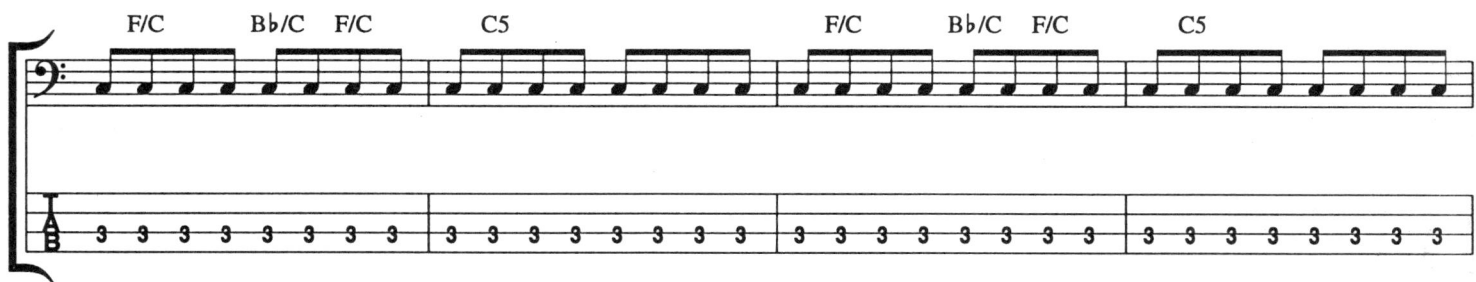
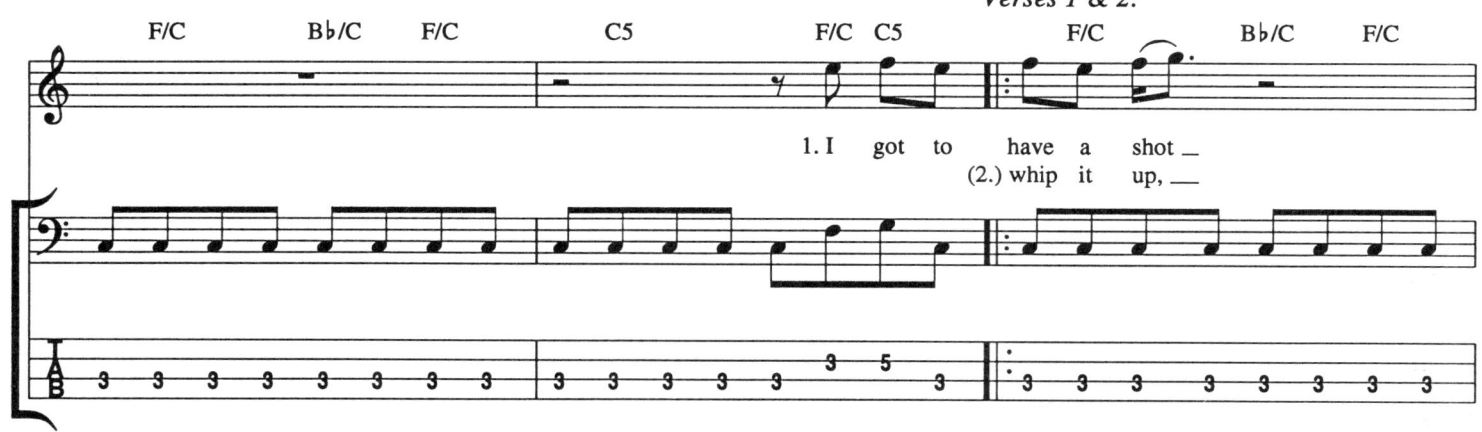

Gimme All Your Lovin' - 5 - 1
P0986BGX

Copyright © 1983, 1992 HAMSTEIN MUSIC COMPANY (ASCAP)
International Copyright Secured   Made In U.S.A.   All Rights Reserved   Used by Permission

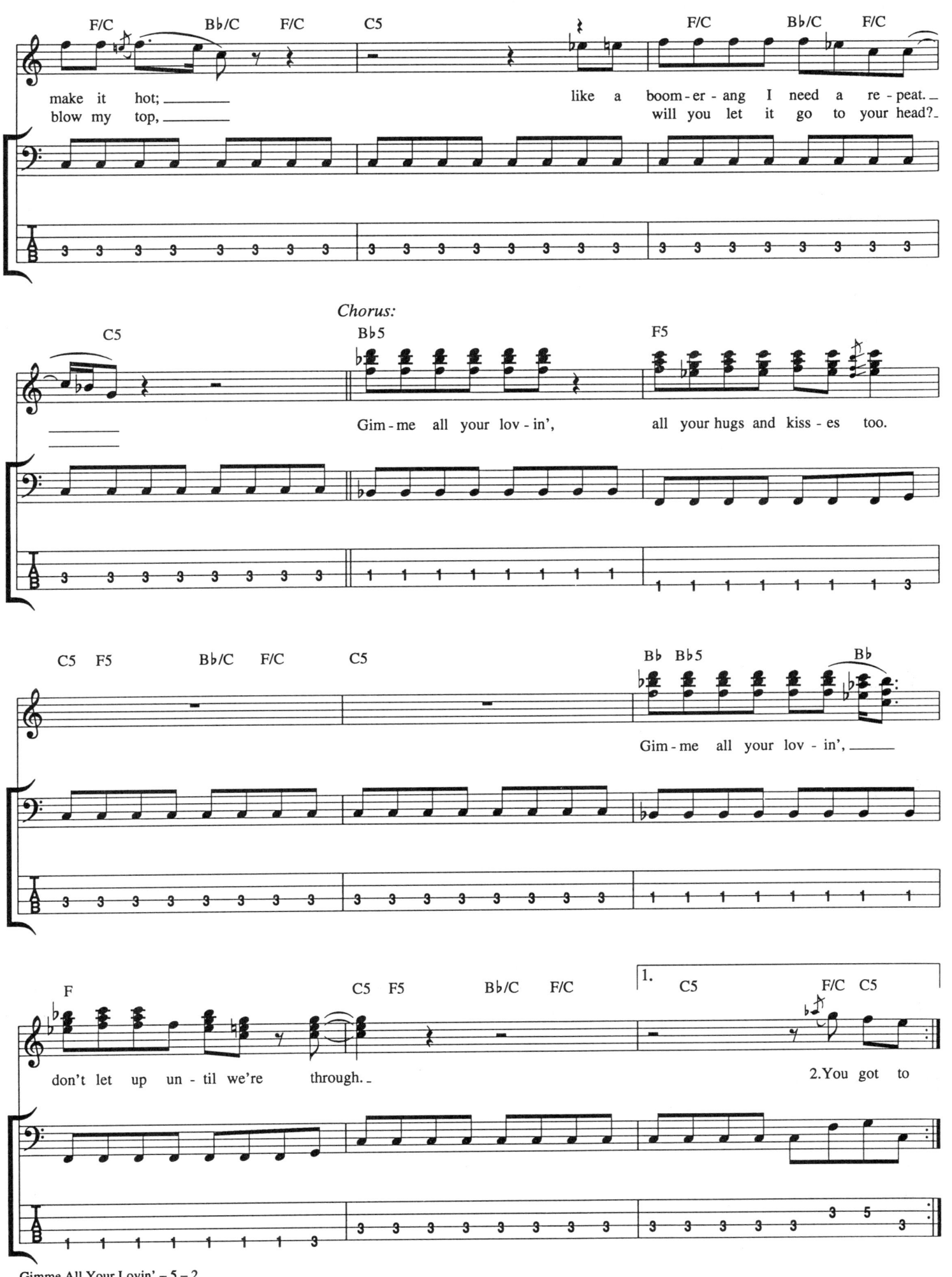

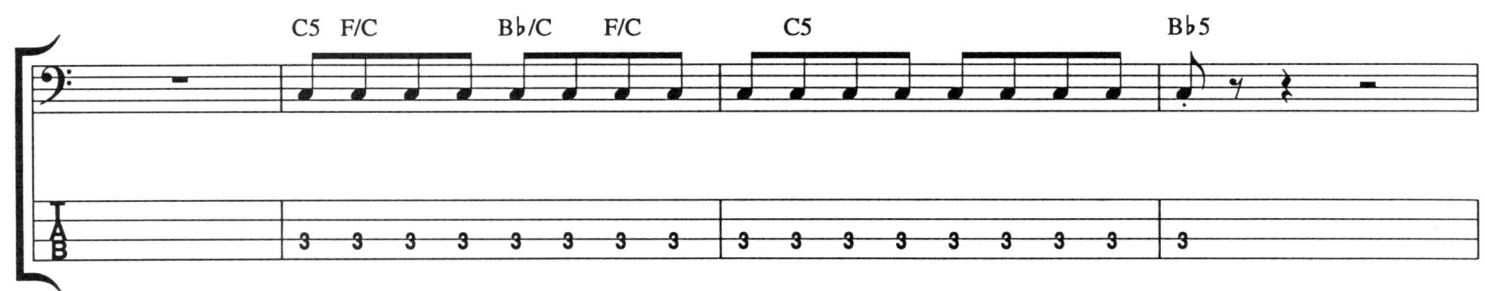

Gimme All Your Lovin' - 5 - 3
P0986BGX

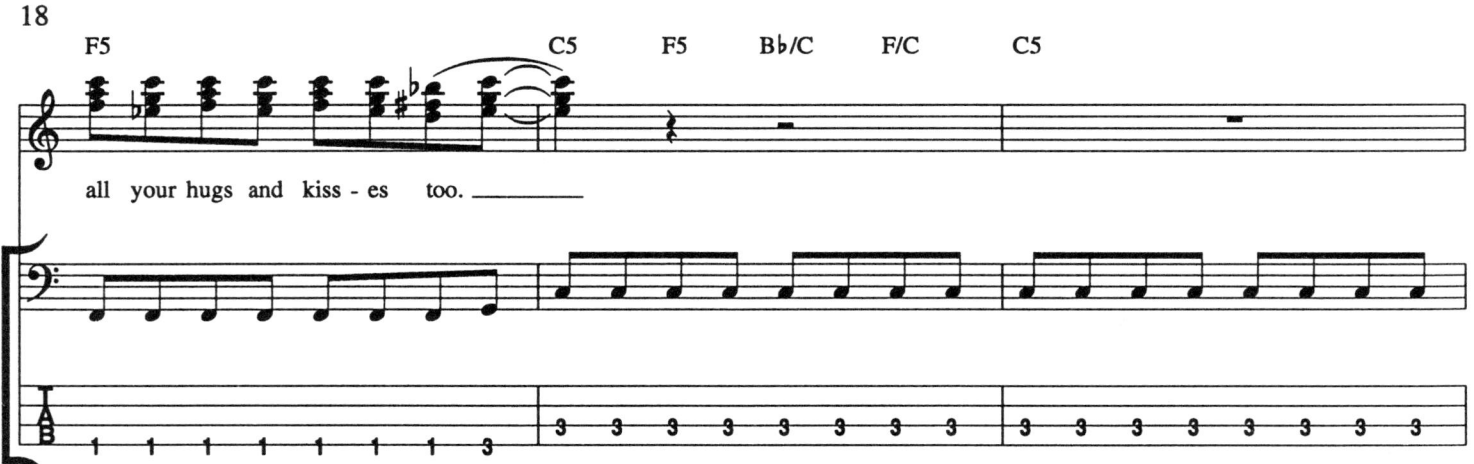

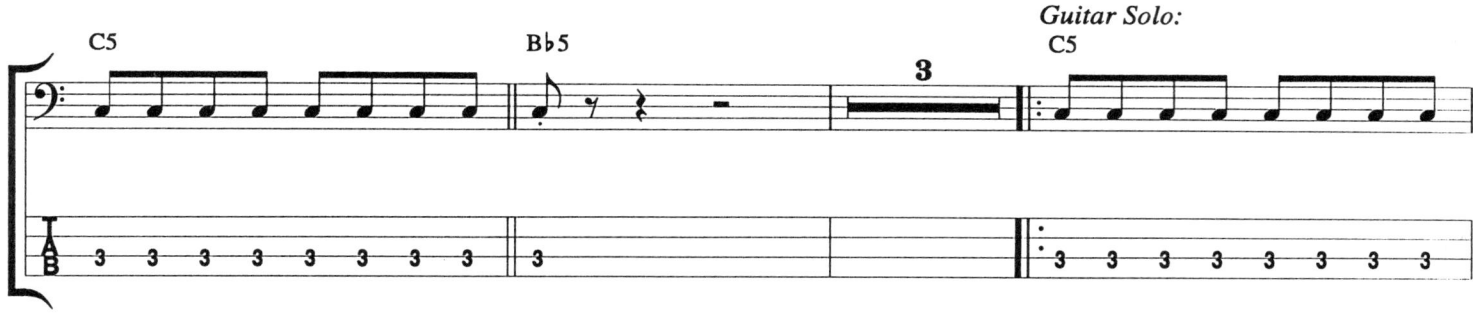
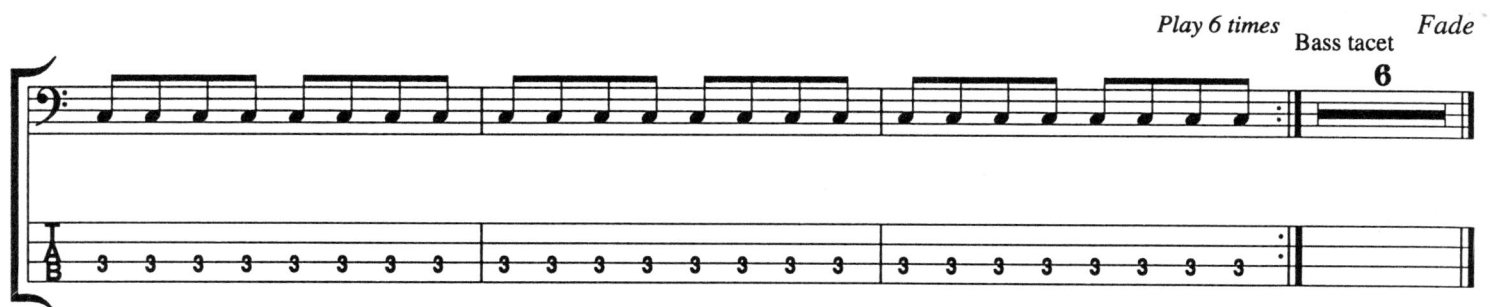

I'M BAD, I'M NATIONWIDE

Words and Music by
BILLY GIBBONS, DUSTY HILL
and FRANK BEARD

21

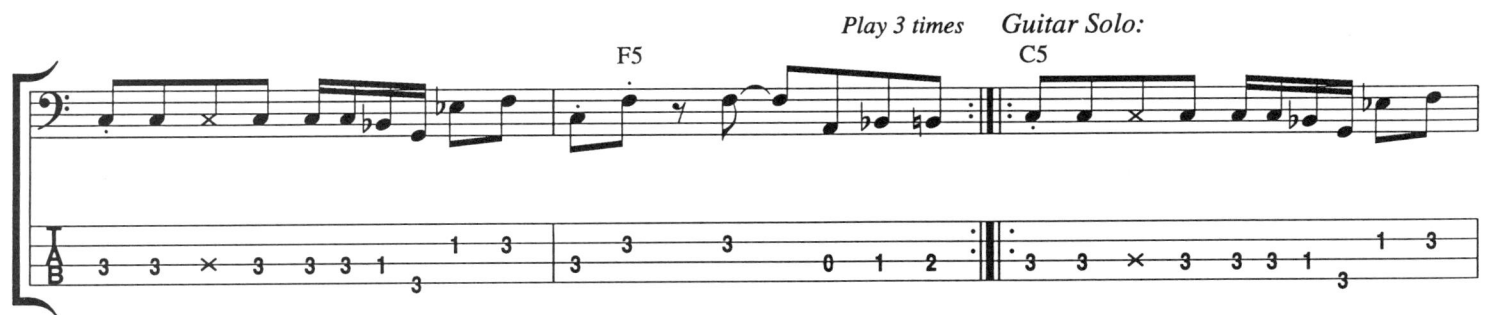

I'm Bad, I'm Nationwide – 5 – 3
P0986BGX

I'm Bad, I'm Nationwide – 5 – 4
P0986BGX

Verse 3:
Well, I was moving down the road
In my V-Eight Ford.
I had a shine on my boots,
I had my sideburns lowered.
With my New York brim
And my gold tooth displayed,
Nobody give me trouble
'Cause they know I got it made.

Chorus 3:
I'm bad, I'm nationwide.
Well, I'm bad, bad, bad, bad, bad,
I'm nationwide.

I'm Bad, I'm Nationwide – 5 – 5
P0986BGX

GIVE IT UP

Words and Music by
BILLY GIBBONS, DUSTY HILL
and FRANK BEARD

Give It Up – 4 – 1
P0986BGX

Copyright © 1990 HAMSTEIN MUSIC COMPANY (ASCAP)
International Copyright Secured   Made In U.S.A.   All Rights Reserved   Used by Permission

25

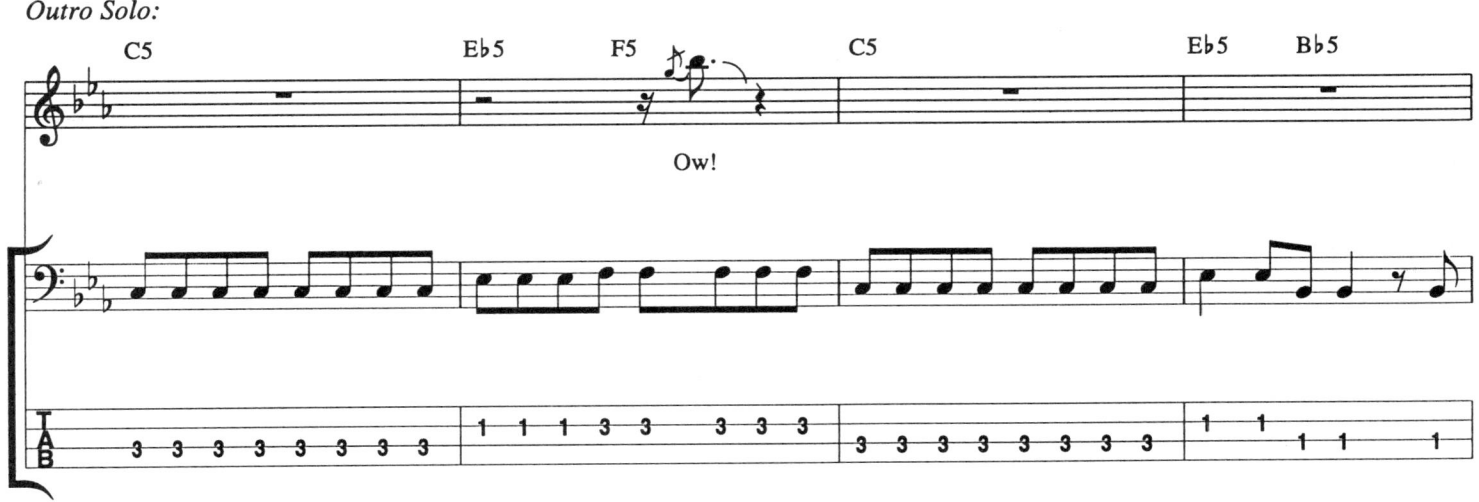
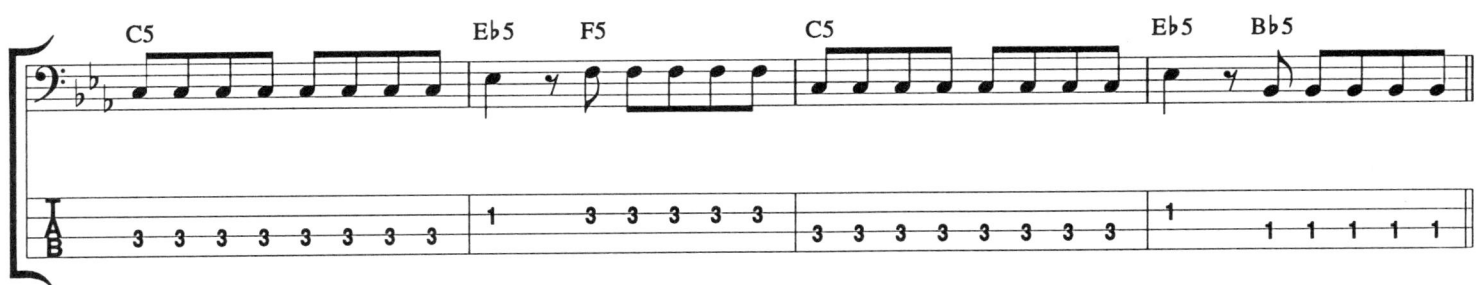
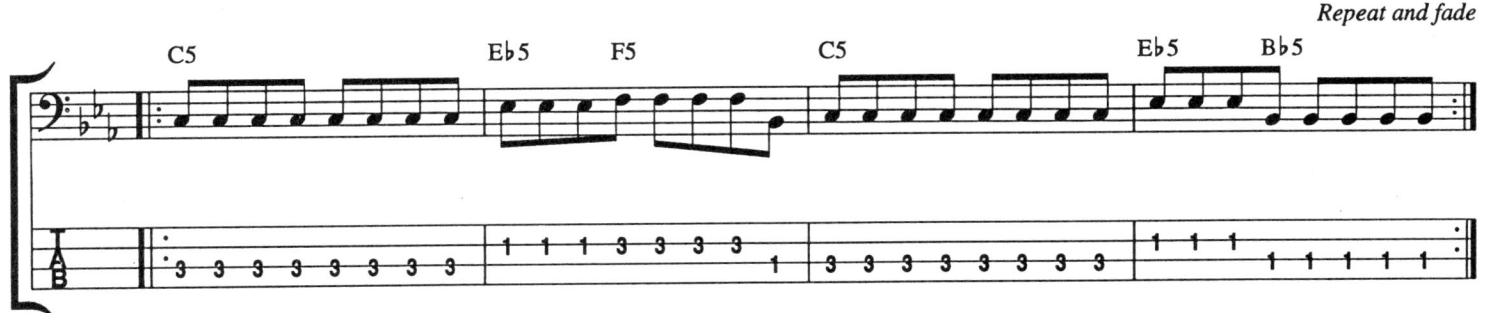

Verse 3:
I fell in love down in Mexico.
Thunderbird Wine's the only way to go.
I been in love 10,000 times,
All you gotta do is remember my lines.
(To Chorus:)

GOT ME UNDER PRESSURE

Words and Music by
BILLY GIBBONS, DUSTY HILL
and FRANK BEARD

*Bass doubled by synth one octave lower throughout.

Got Me Under Pressure - 6 - 1
P0986BGX

Copyright © 1983 HAMSTEIN MUSIC COMPANY (ASCAP)
International Copyright Secured   Made In U.S.A.   All Rights Reserved   Used by Permission

30 *Verse 2:*

w/Bass Fig. 1 *(9 1/2 times)*

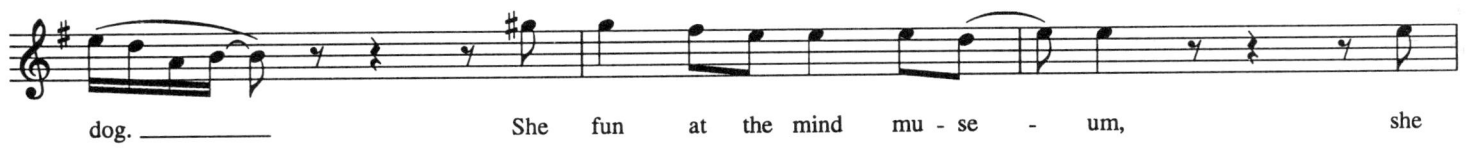

Got Me Under Pressure – 6 – 3
P0986BGX

Got Me Under Pressure – 6 – 4
P0986BGX

LA GRANGE

ROUGH BOY

F#m7
E/F#
Bm7
one in three. _ Ain't got no rap, ___ ain't got no line, _ but if you'll
1.
E
Esus
give me just a min - ute I'll be feel - ing fine. _
2. 3.
E
give me just a min - ute and I'll
Chorus:
A
E/A
A
E/A
tell you why. _ I'm a rough boy. ___ I'm a
A
E/A
E7sus
Guitar Solo:
C#m
rough boy. ___

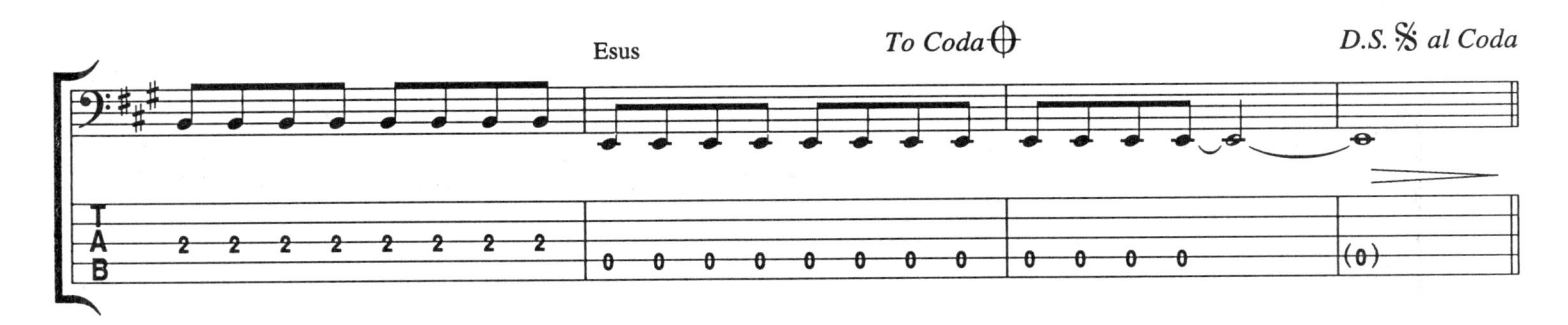

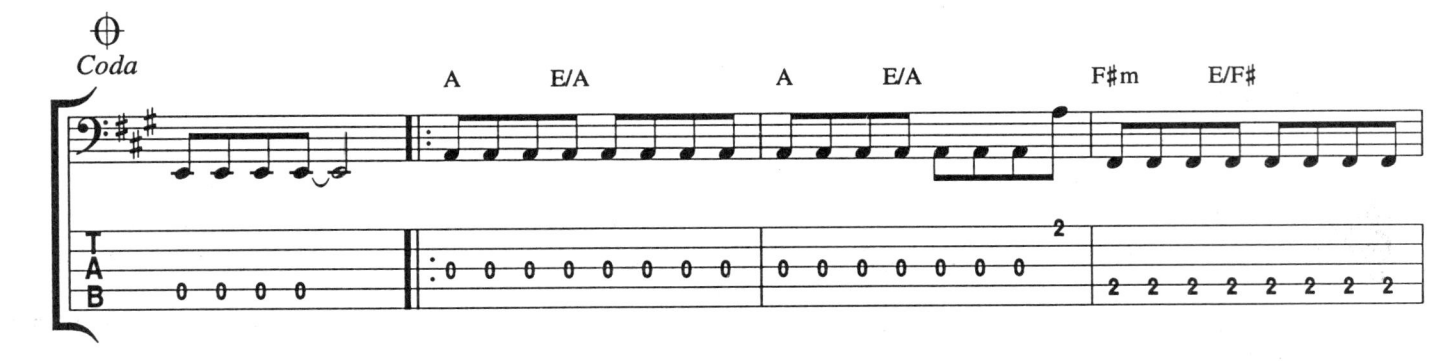

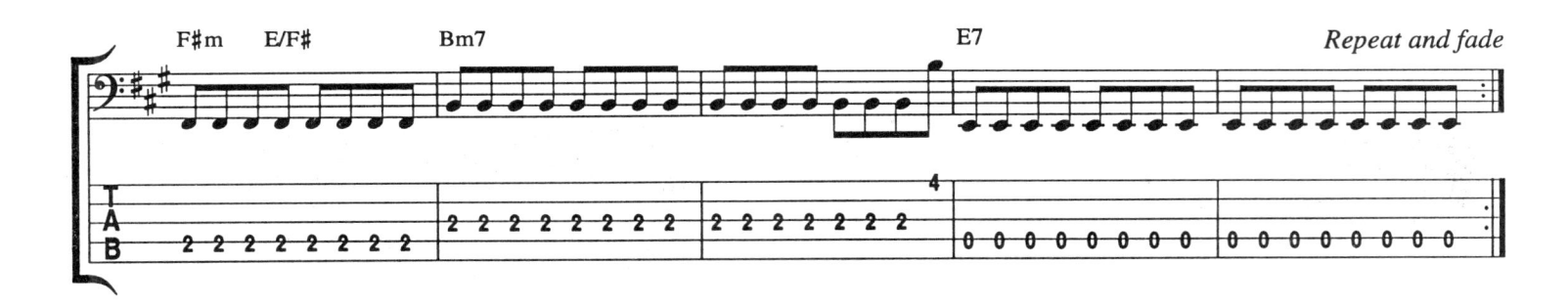

Verse 2:
I am the one who can fade the heat;
The one they all say just can't be beat.
I'll shoot it to you straight
And look you in the eye.
So give me just a minute
And I'll tell you why . . .
(To Chorus:)

Verse 3:
I don't care how you look at me,
Because I'm the one and you will see.
We can make it work,
We can make it by,
So give me one more minute
And I'll tell you why . . .
(To Chorus:)

SLEEPING BAG

Words and Music by
BILLY GIBBONS, DUSTY HILL
and FRANK BEARD

40

sleep-in' bag. Slip in-side my sleep-in' bag. 2. You're a-

sleep - in' bag.

Guitar Solo:

Play 4 times

Sleeping Bag – 3 – 2
P0986BGX

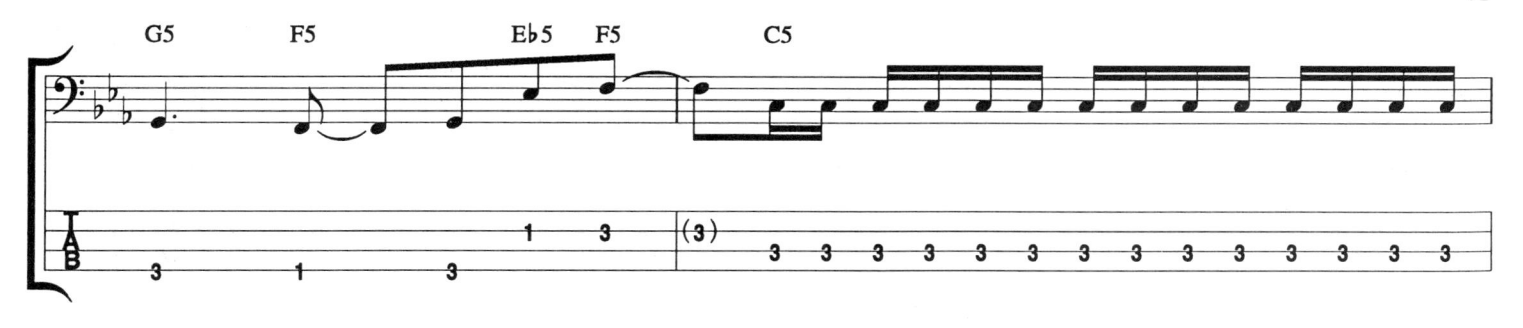

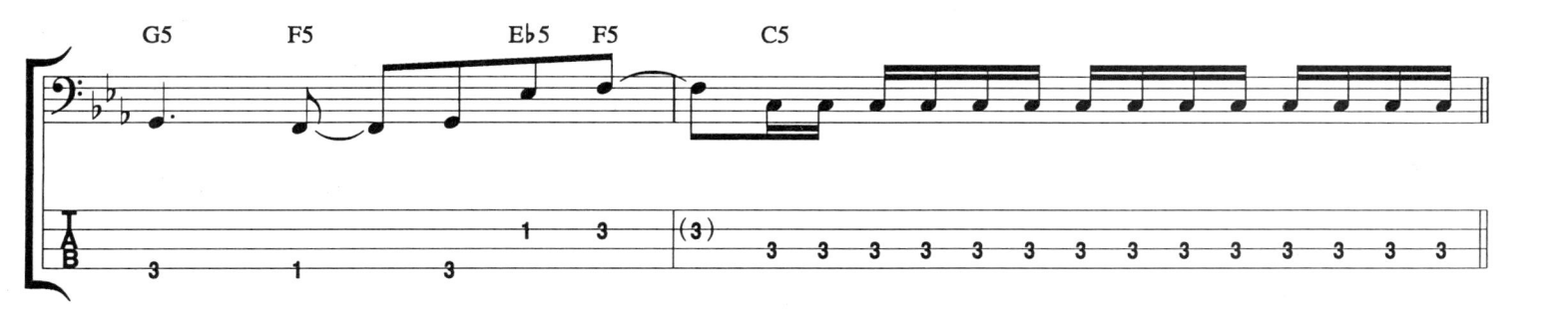

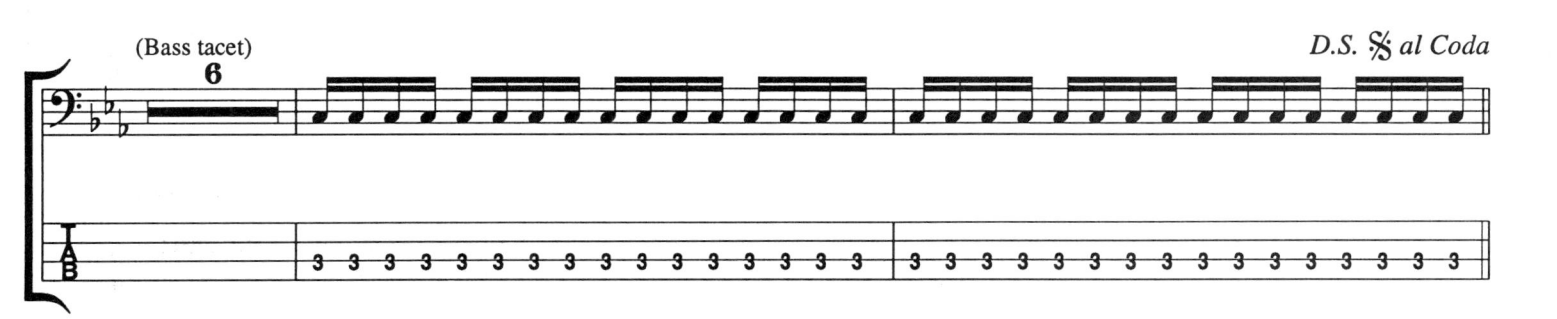

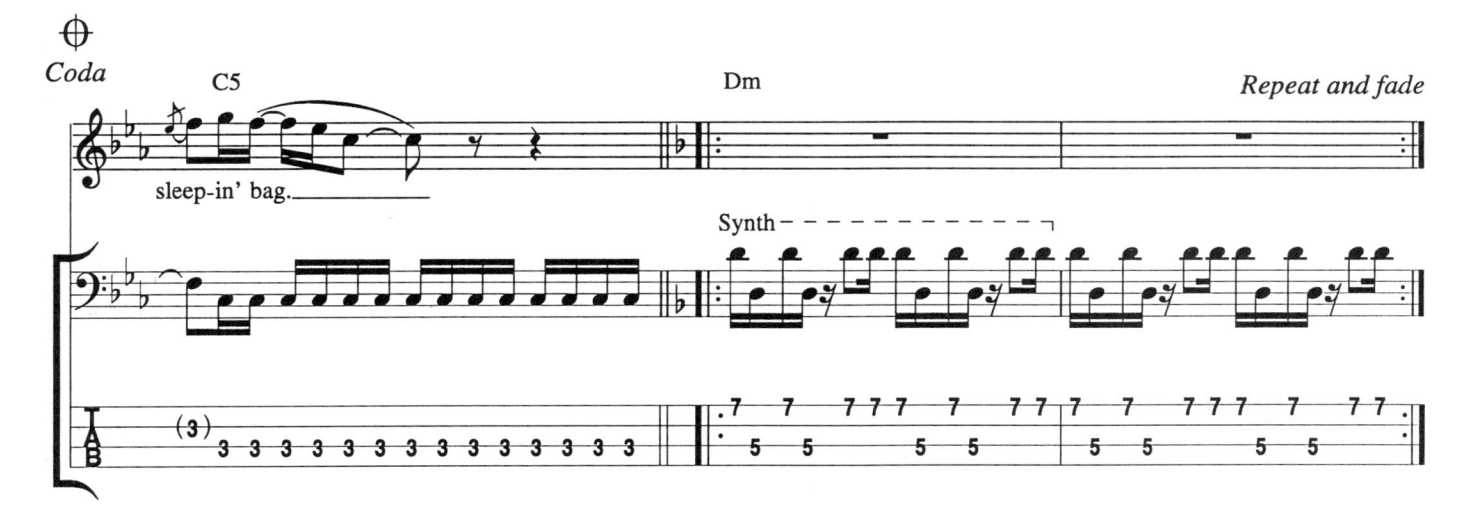

Verse 3:
Let's go out to Egypt 'cause it's in the plan,
Sleep beside the Pharaohs in the shifting sand.
We'll look at some pyramids and check out some heads,
Gonna whip out our mattress 'cause there ain't no beds.
(To Chorus:)

SHARP DRESSED MAN

Words and Music by
BILLY GIBBONS, DUSTY HILL
and FRANK BEARD

Moderately fast ♩ = 124

F5 G5
I don't need a rea - son why. They come run - nin' just as
To Coda
C5
fast as they can, 'cause ev - ery girl cra - zy 'bout a
1. Eb5 Bb5 C5 F5 Eb C5 F5 Eb C5
sharp dressed man.
F5 Eb C5 F5 Eb C5
2. Eb5 Bb5
Sharp dressed man.

Guitar Solo:
C5
Play 4 times
B♭5 G5
F5
C5
F5
C5
B♭5 G5
C5 F5 E♭5 C5 F5 E♭5 C5 F5 E♭5 C5 F5 E♭5 C5
T
A
B

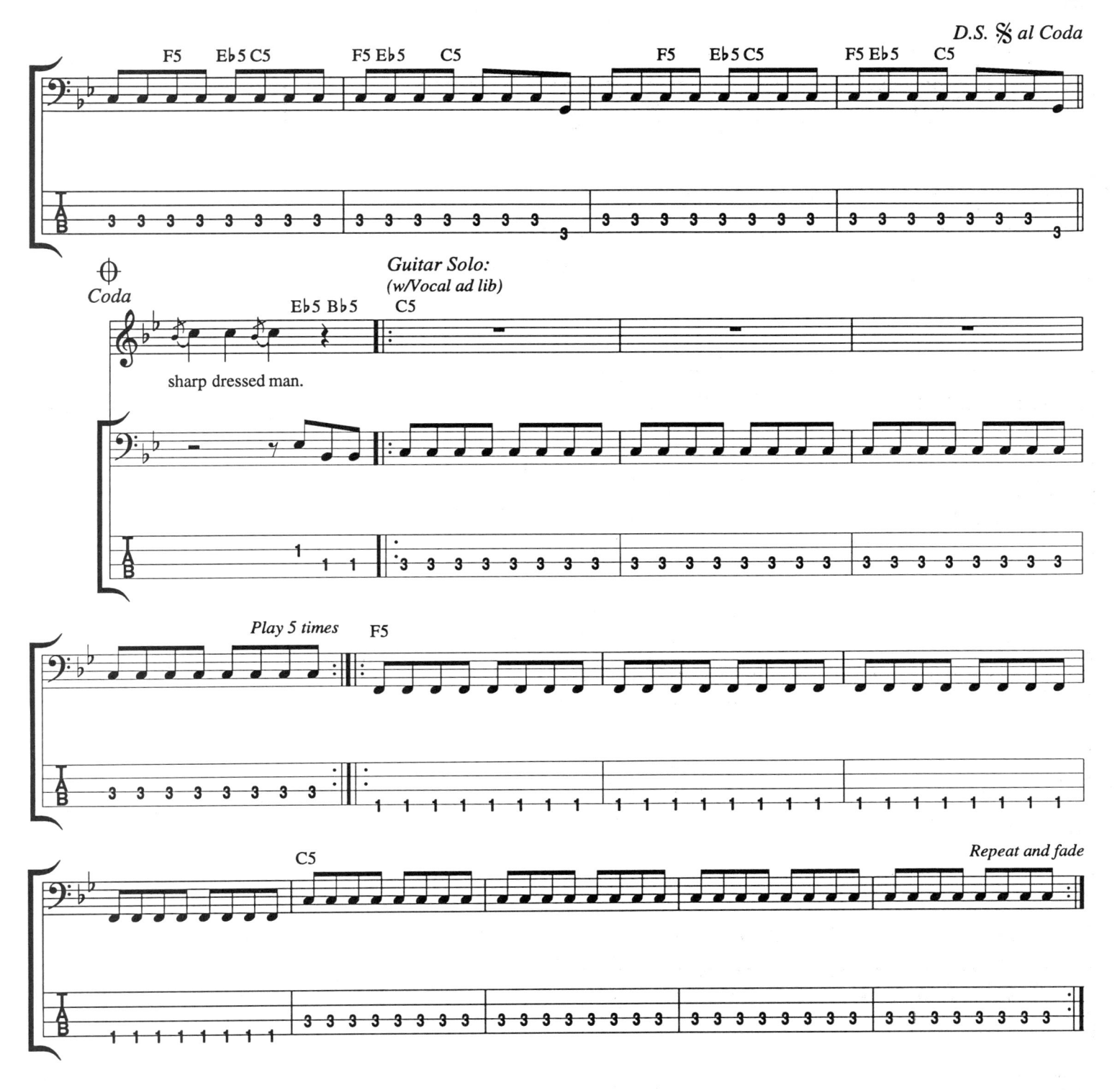

Verse 2:
Gold watch, diamond ring,
I ain't missin' not a single thing.
Cuff links, stick pin,
When I step out I'm gonna do you in.
They come runnin' just as fast as they can,
'Cause every girl crazy 'bout a sharp dressed man.
(To Guitar Solo:)

Verse 3:
Top coat, top hat,
I don't worry 'cause my wallet's fat.
Black shades, white gloves,
Lookin' sharp and lookin' for love.
They come runnin' just as fast as they can,
'Cause every girl crazy 'bout a sharp dressed man.
(To Coda)

STAGES

Words and Music by
BILLY GIBBONS, DUSTY HILL
and FRANK BEARD

Moderately fast rock ♩ = 156

Intro:

1. It's a fine time to fall in love with you.
2. Then you left me standin' all alone.
3. *See additional lyrics.*

I _____ ain't got a sin-
I could-n't e - ven get

Em7 D/E
- gle thing to do. It hap -
you on the phone. Were
G D/G G D/G
- pened be - fore I knew what was go - ing on.
you just con - fused and did - n't know
Em7 D/E
I fell out and knew that I was gone.
if you should stay or if you had to go?
Em7 D/E
Chorus:
Csus C Csus
Sta - ges keep

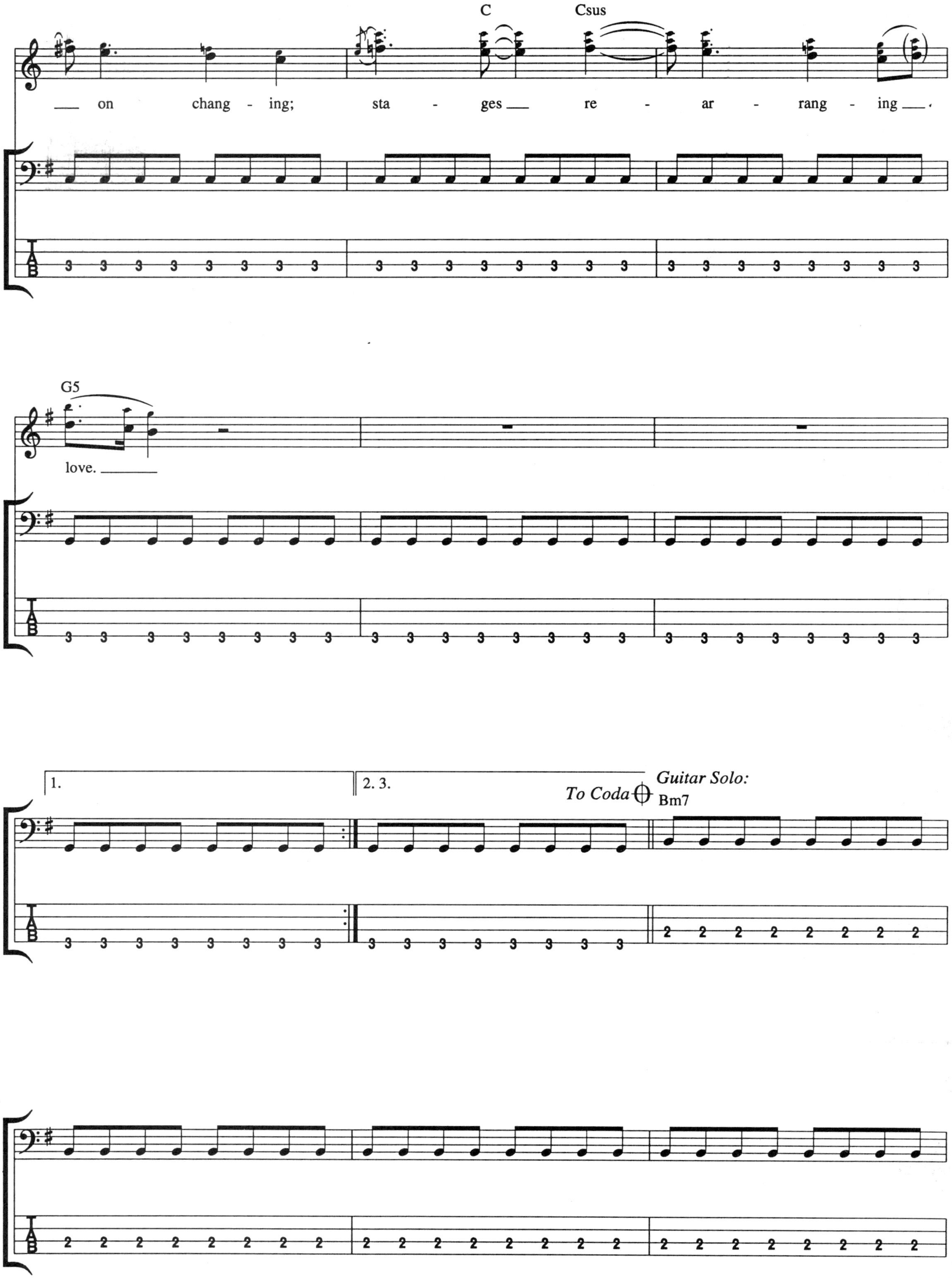
C
Csus
on changing; stages rearranging
G5
love.
1.
2. 3.
To Coda
Guitar Solo:
Bm7

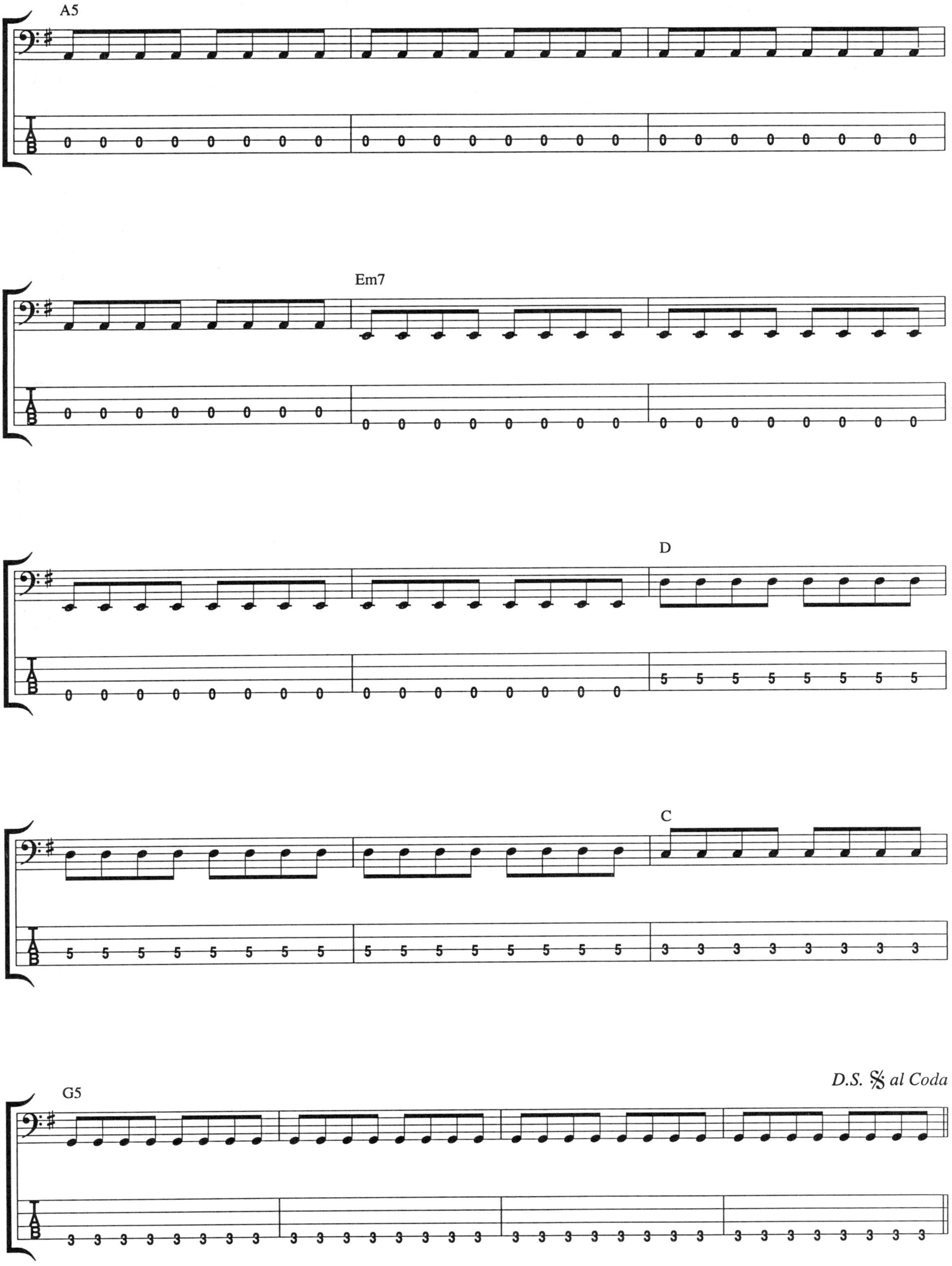
A5
Em7
D
C
G5
D.S. 𝄋 al Coda

Verse 3:
Now you're back and say you're gonna stay.
I wouldn't have it any other way.
Tell me it's for real and let me know;
Why does lovin' have to come and go?
(To Chorus:)

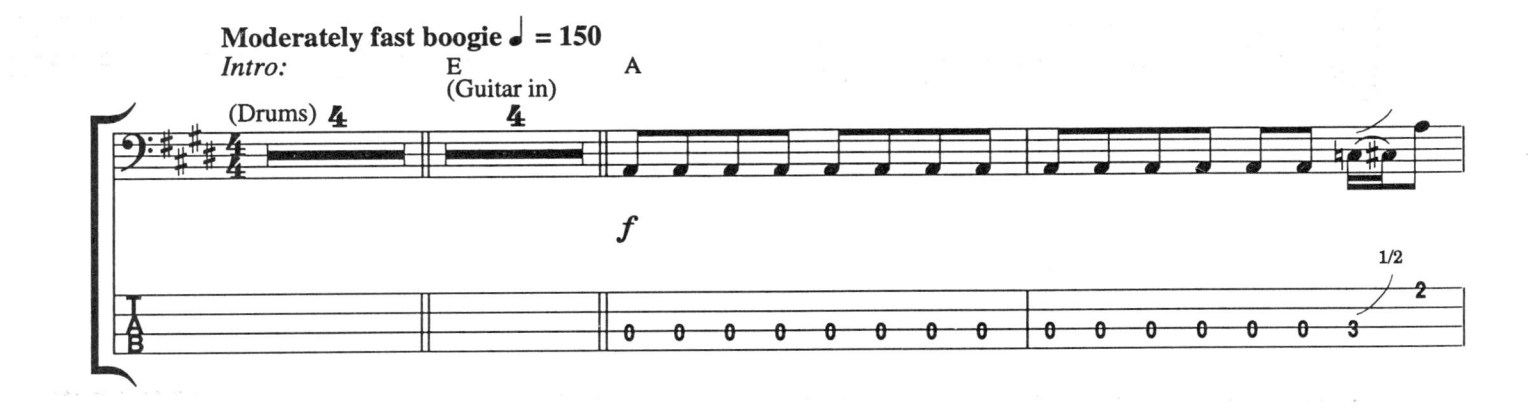

TUBE SNAKE BOOGIE

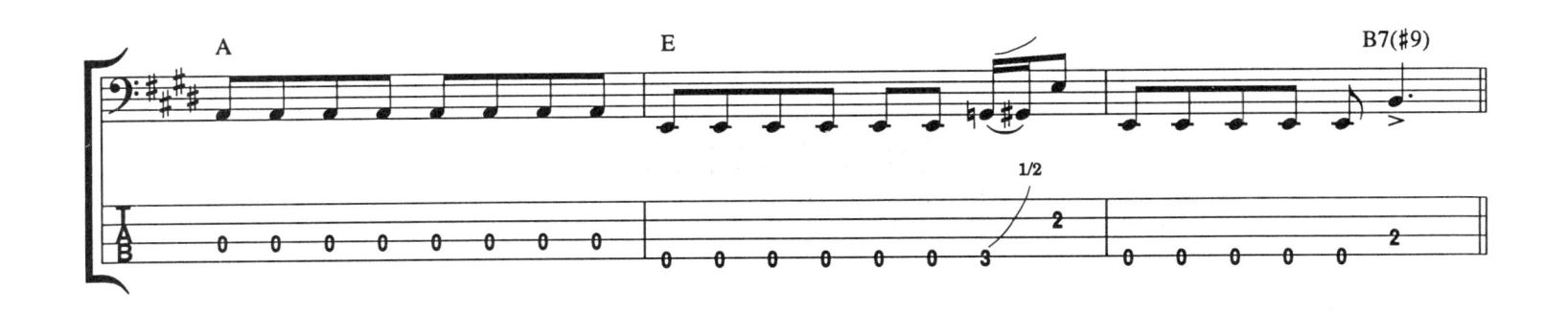

Words and Music by
BILLY GIBBONS, DUSTY HILL
and FRANK BEARD

Verses 1 & 2:

1. I got a gal, she lives cross town, she's the one that real-ly gets down. When she boo-gie, she do the tube snake boo-gie. Well, now boo-gie lit-tle ba-by, boo-gie woo-gie all night long.

2. *(See additional lyrics)*

Bass Fig. 1

(end Bass Fig. 1)

Tube Snake Boogie – 5 – 2
P0986BGX

Guitar Solo:

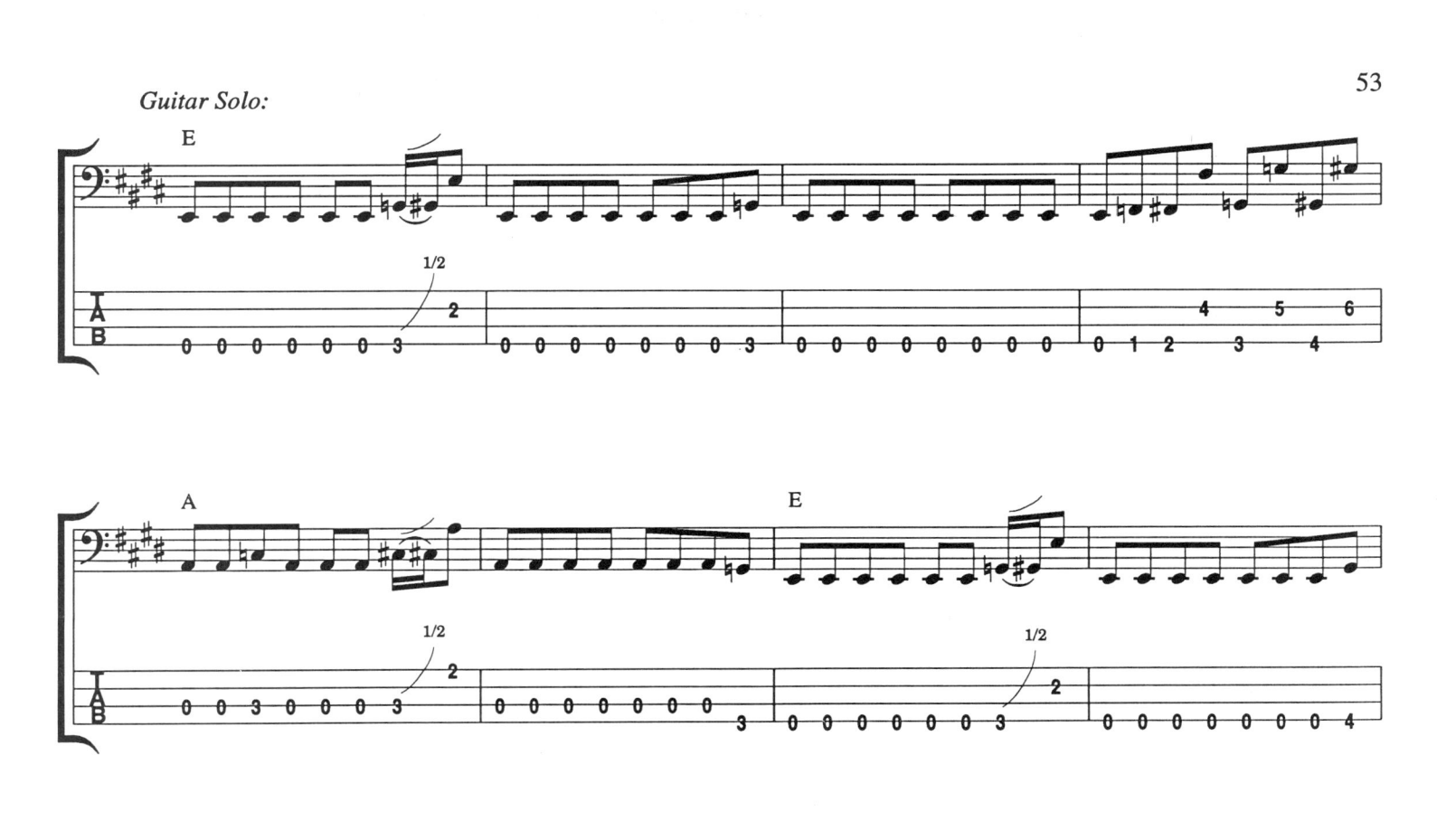

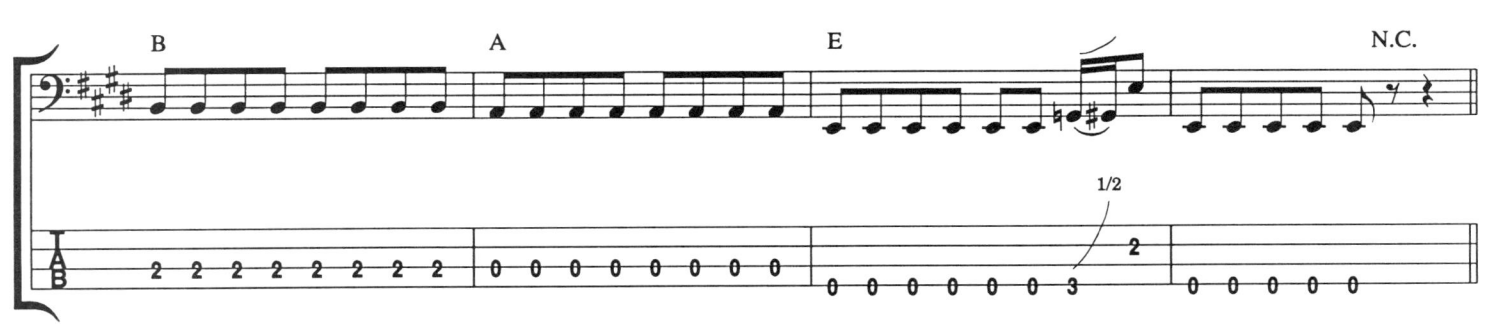

Tube Snake Boogie – 5 – 3
P0986BGX

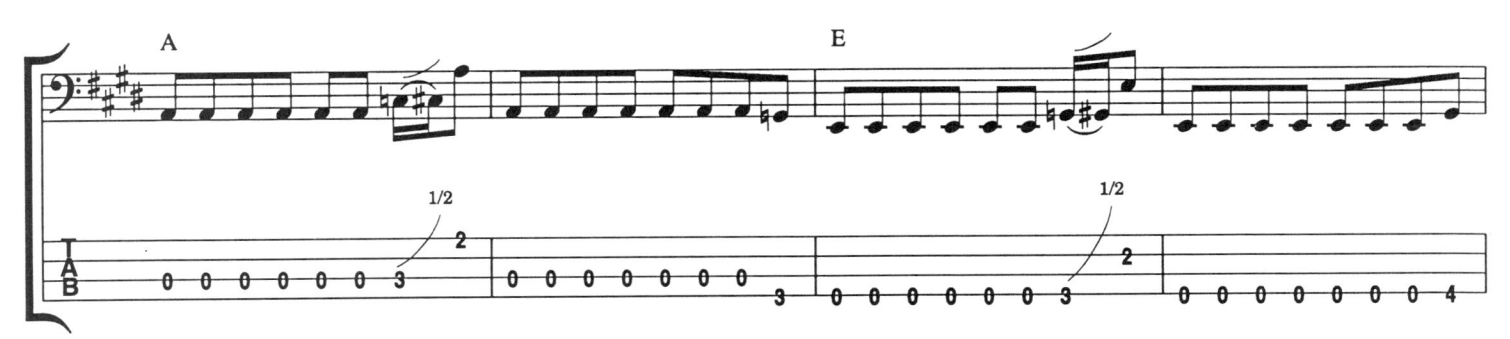

54

Verse 3:

I got a gal, she lives on the hill. She won't do it but her sister will. When she boo-gie, she do the tube snake boo-gie.

Well, now boo-gie lit-tle ba-by,

*Voice chorused 1 octave higher

Tube Snake boogie – 5 – 4
P0986BGX

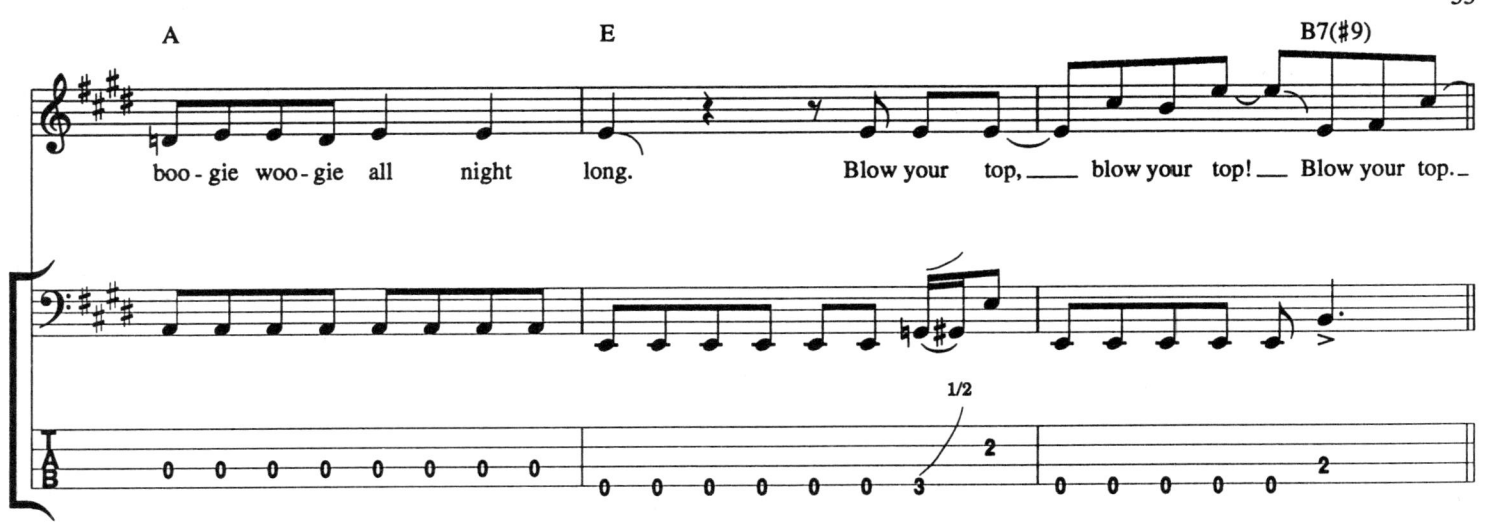

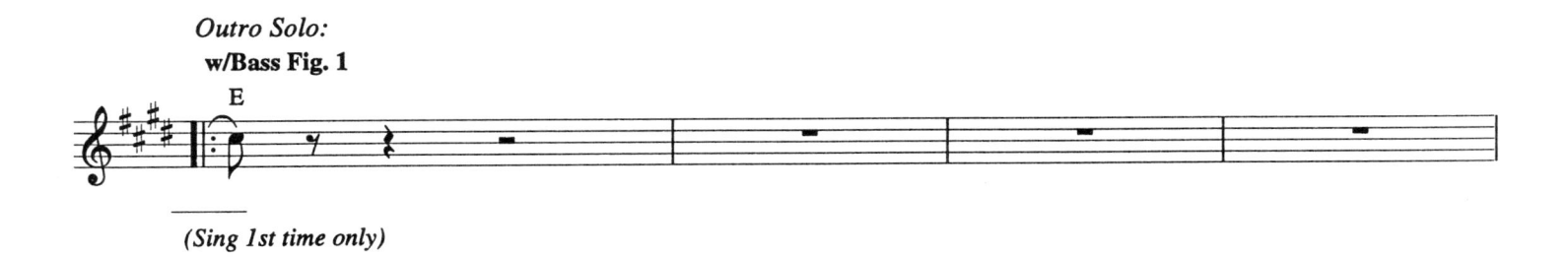

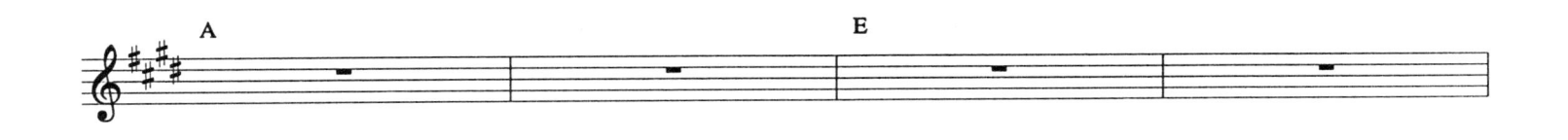

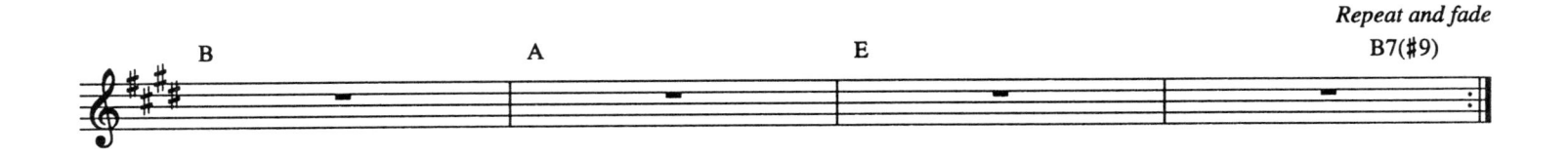

Verse 2:
I got a gal, she lives on the block.
She kind of funky with her pink and black socks.
She likes to boogie,
She do the tube snake boogie.
Well, now boogie woogie baby,
Boogie woogie all night long.

TUSH

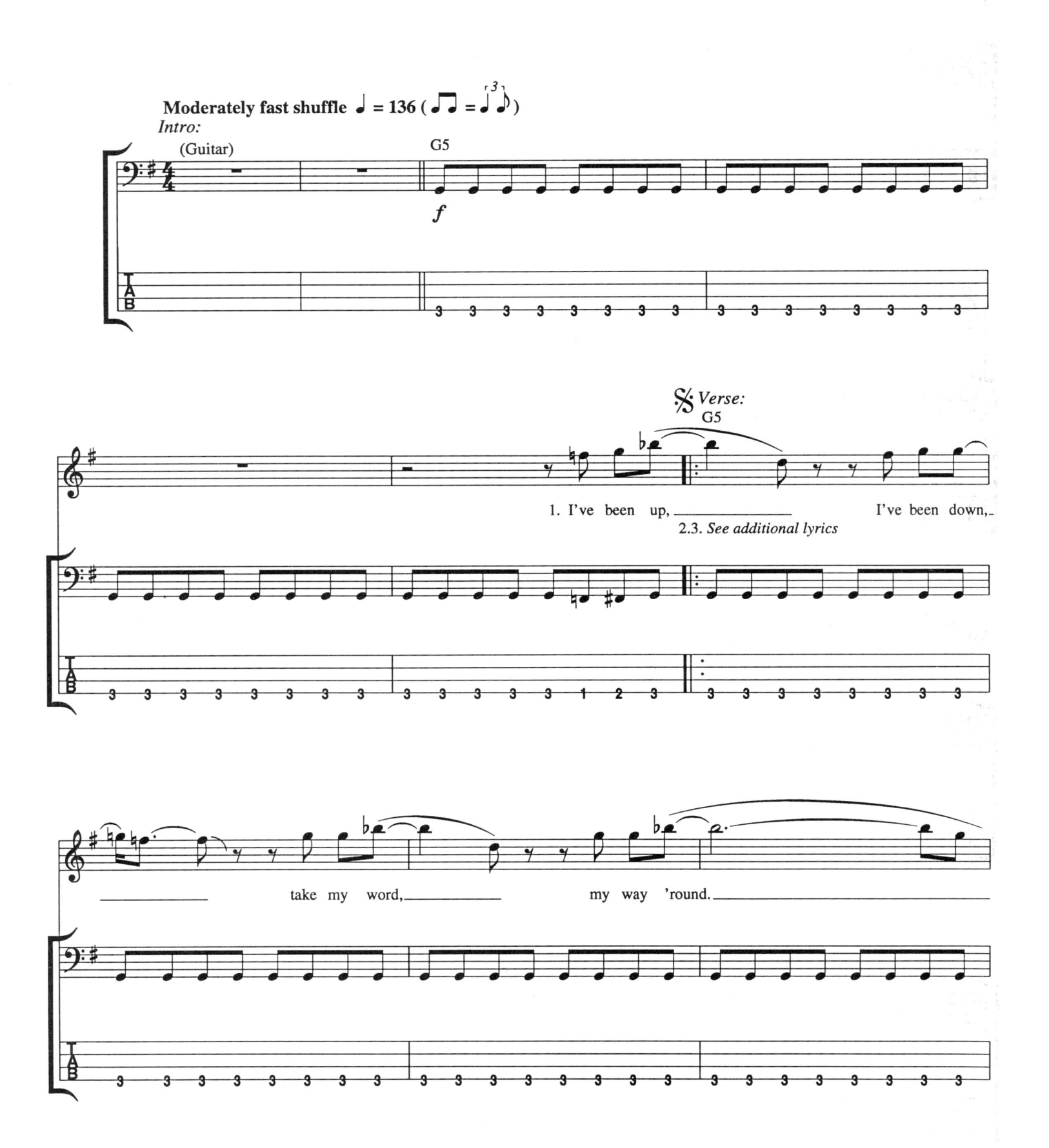

Words and Music by
BILLY GIBBONS, DUSTY HILL
and FRANK BEARD

Moderately fast shuffle ♩ = 136

Intro: (Guitar)

Verse:
1. I've been up, I've been down, take my word, my way 'round.
2.3. *See additional lyrics*

57

Tush – 3 – 2
P0986BGX

Verse 2:
I've been bad; I've been good,
Dallas, Texas; Hollywood.
I ain't asking for much.
I said Lord take me downtown
I'm just looking for some tush.
(To Guitar Solo:)

Verse 3:
Take me back, way back home,
Not by myself; not alone.
I ain't asking for much.
I said Lord take me downtown
I'm just looking for some tush.
(To Coda)

TV DINNERS

5-string bass is tuned:
⑤ = B   ② = D
④ = E   ① = G
③ = A

Words and Music by
BILLY GIBBONS, DUSTY HILL
and FRANK BEARD

Moderate ♩ = 99

*Synth bass arr. for 5-string bass.

1. TV dinners;
2.3. *See additional lyrics.*

there's nothing else to eat.

TV dinners; they really can't be

TV Dinners - 5 - 1
P0986BGX

Copyright © 1983 HAMSTEIN MUSIC COMPANY (ASCAP)
All Rights Reserved   Made In U.S.A.   International Copyright Secured   Used by Permission

B5
beat.
Oh, I like 'em froz - en, but you
To Coda
un - der - stand.
I throw 'em in and 'wave 'em and I'm a brand new man, oh yeah.
D5
1.
2.
N.C.
2. T V

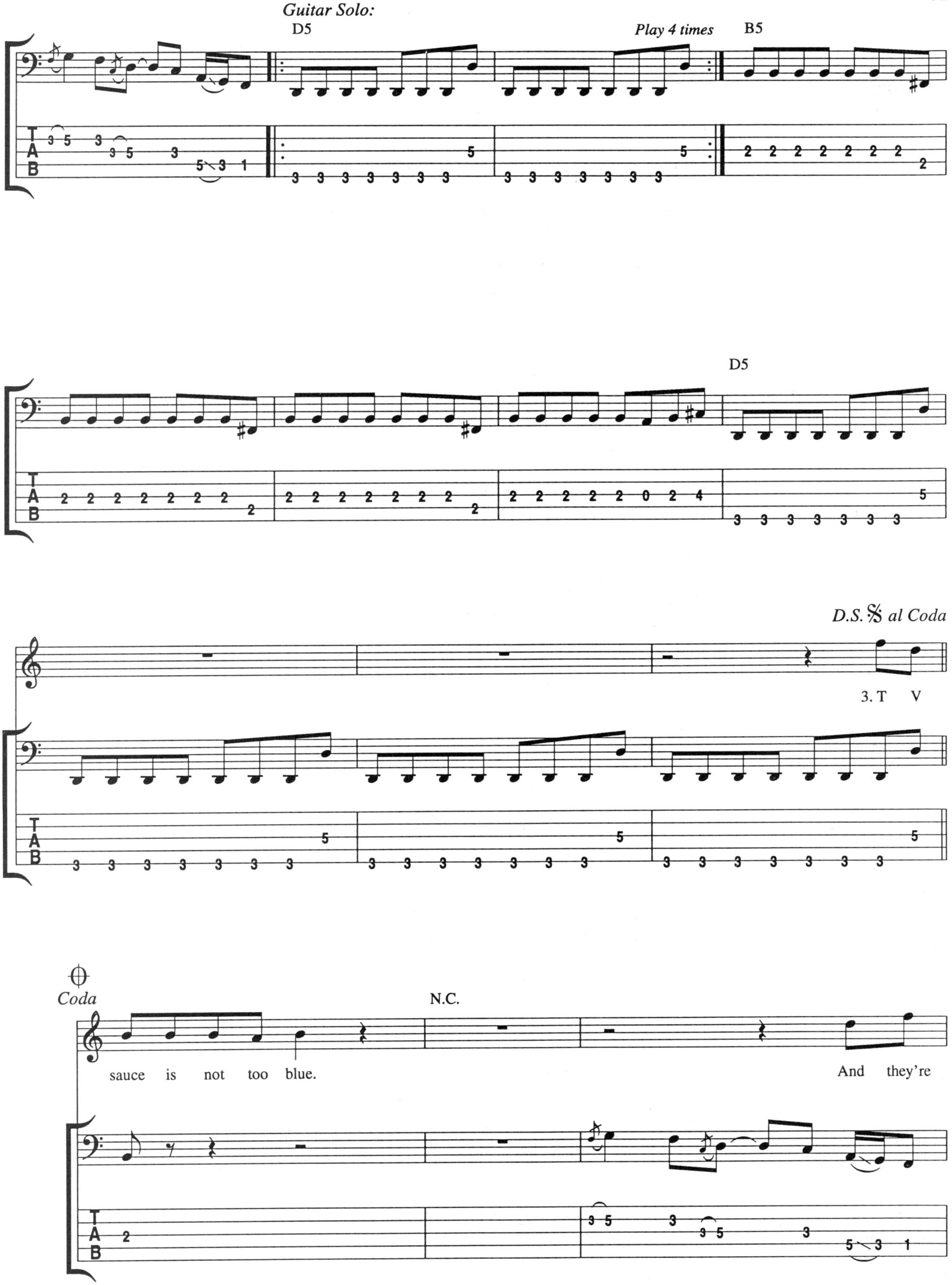
Guitar Solo:
D5
Play 4 times
B5
D5
D.S. al Coda
3. T V
Coda
N.C.
sauce is not too blue.
And they're

mine, all mine,___ oh yeah.___

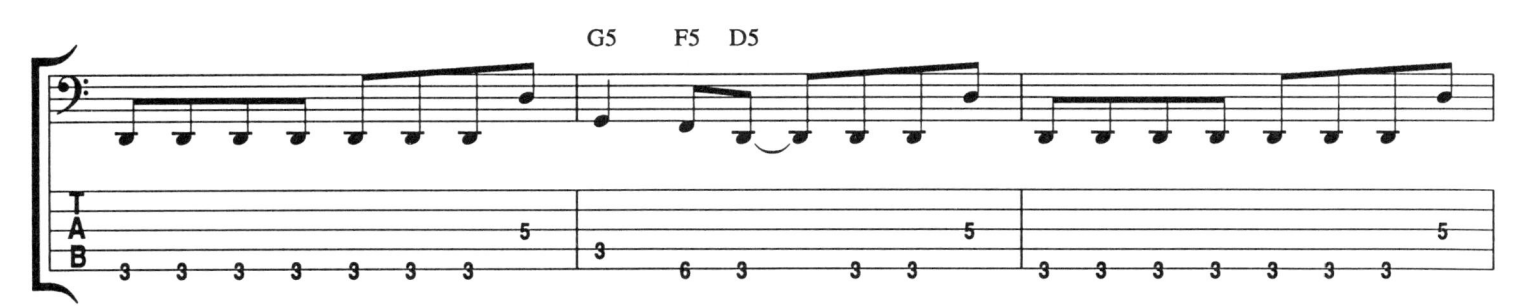

And they sure are fine,___ whoa,

got-ta have 'em. gim-me some-thin' now, hon-ey.

TV Dinners – 5 – 4
P0986BGX

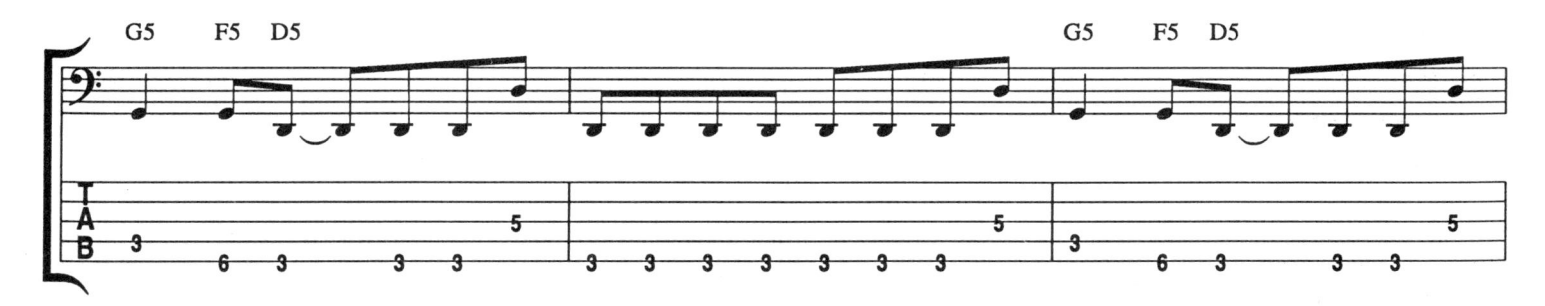

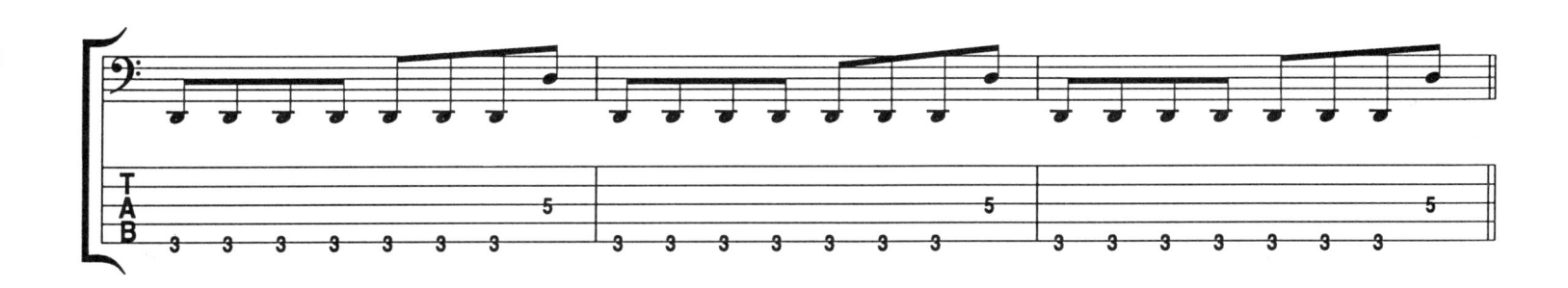

Verse 2:
T V dinners; they're goin' to my head.
T V dinners; my skin is turnin' red.
Twenty year old turkey
In a thirty year old tin.
I can't wait until tomorrow
And thaw one out again, oh yeah.
(To Solo:)

Verse 3:
T V dinners; I'm feelin' kind of rough.
T V dinners; this one's kind of tough.
I like the enchiladas
And the teriyaki, too.
I even like the chicken
If the sauce is not too blue.
(To Coda)

VIVA! LAS VEGAS

Words and Music by
DOC POMUS and MORT SHUMAN

Moderately fast rock ♩ = 120

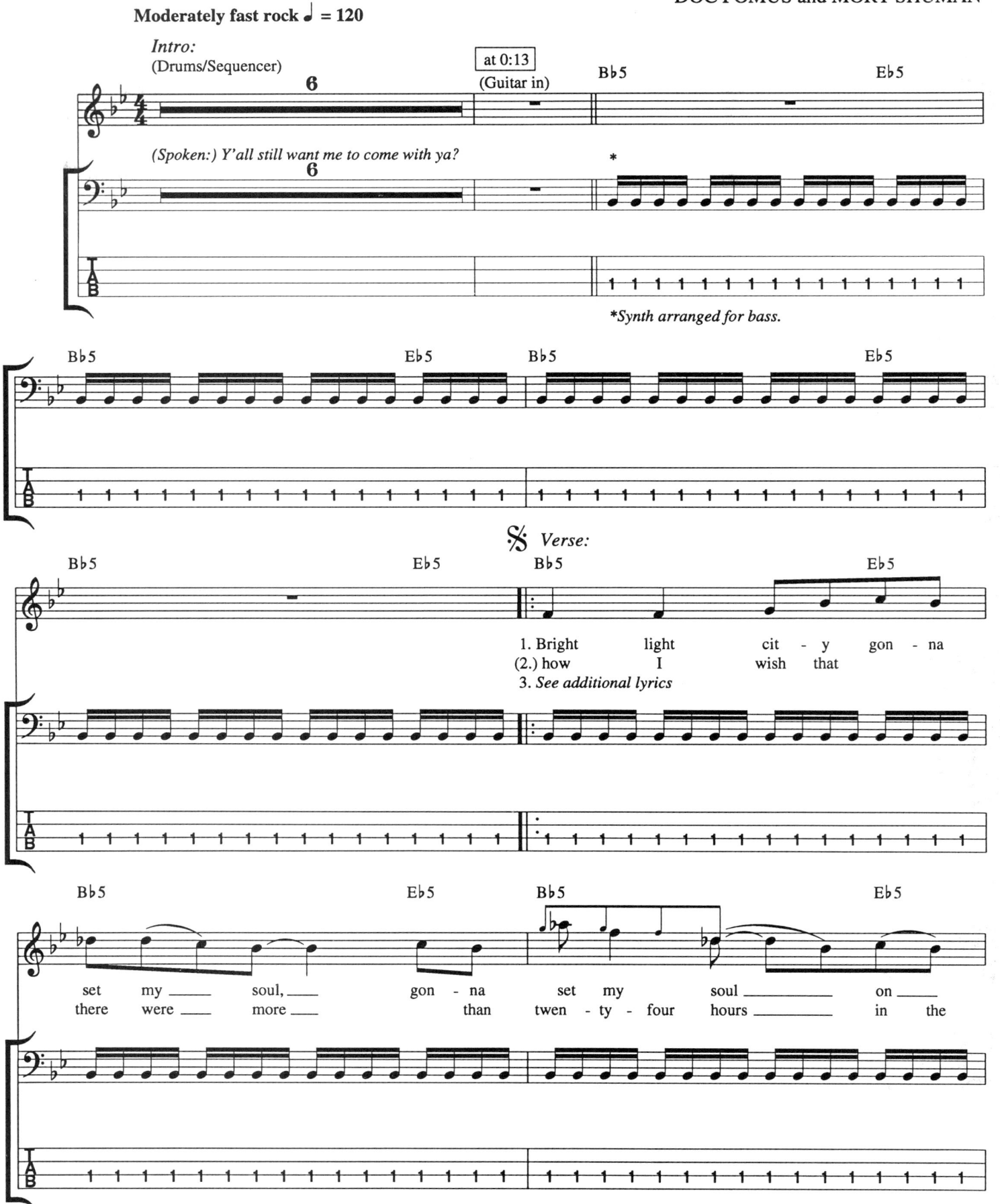

Intro:
(Drums/Sequencer) — at 0:13 (Guitar in)

(Spoken:) Y'all still want me to come with ya?

*Synth arranged for bass.

Verse:

1. Bright light city gonna set my soul, gonna set my soul on
(2.) how I wish that there were more than twenty-four hours in the
3. *See additional lyrics*

© 1964 Elvis Presley Music, Inc. (BMI)
Copyright Renewed 1992 by Sharyn Felder & Geoffrey J. Felder
Administered in the U.S. by Pomus Songs, Inc. (N.Y.)
All Rights Reserved International Copyright Secured

Bb5
(echo)
Eb5
fire. (fire) There's a whole lot of mon - ey that's - a -
day. (day) But e - ven if there were
Bb5
Eb5
Bb5
Eb5
read - y to burn so get those stakes up
for - ty more I would - n't sleep a min - ute a - way.
Bb5
G5
high. (high) There's a thou - sand pret - ty wom - en that's - a
(a - way.) Oh, there's black - jack, po - ker and a
wait - in' out there They're all liv - in'
rou - lette wheel. A for - tune won and lost on - a
T
A
B

66

67

Ah, thank you ver-y much, peo-ple. 2. Oh, Vi - va Las Vegas, Vi - va Las Vegas, Las Vegas.

To Coda ✛ *Bridge:*

Vi - va Las Ve - gas with your ne - on flash - in' and your one arm ban - dits crash - in'

Viva! Las Vegas – 7 – 4
P0986BGX

all those hopes down the drain. Vi - va Las Ve - gas, turn - in' day in - to night - time, turn - in' night in - to day - time and you see it once, you nev - er come home a - gain.

Viva! Las Vegas – 7 – 6
P0986BGX

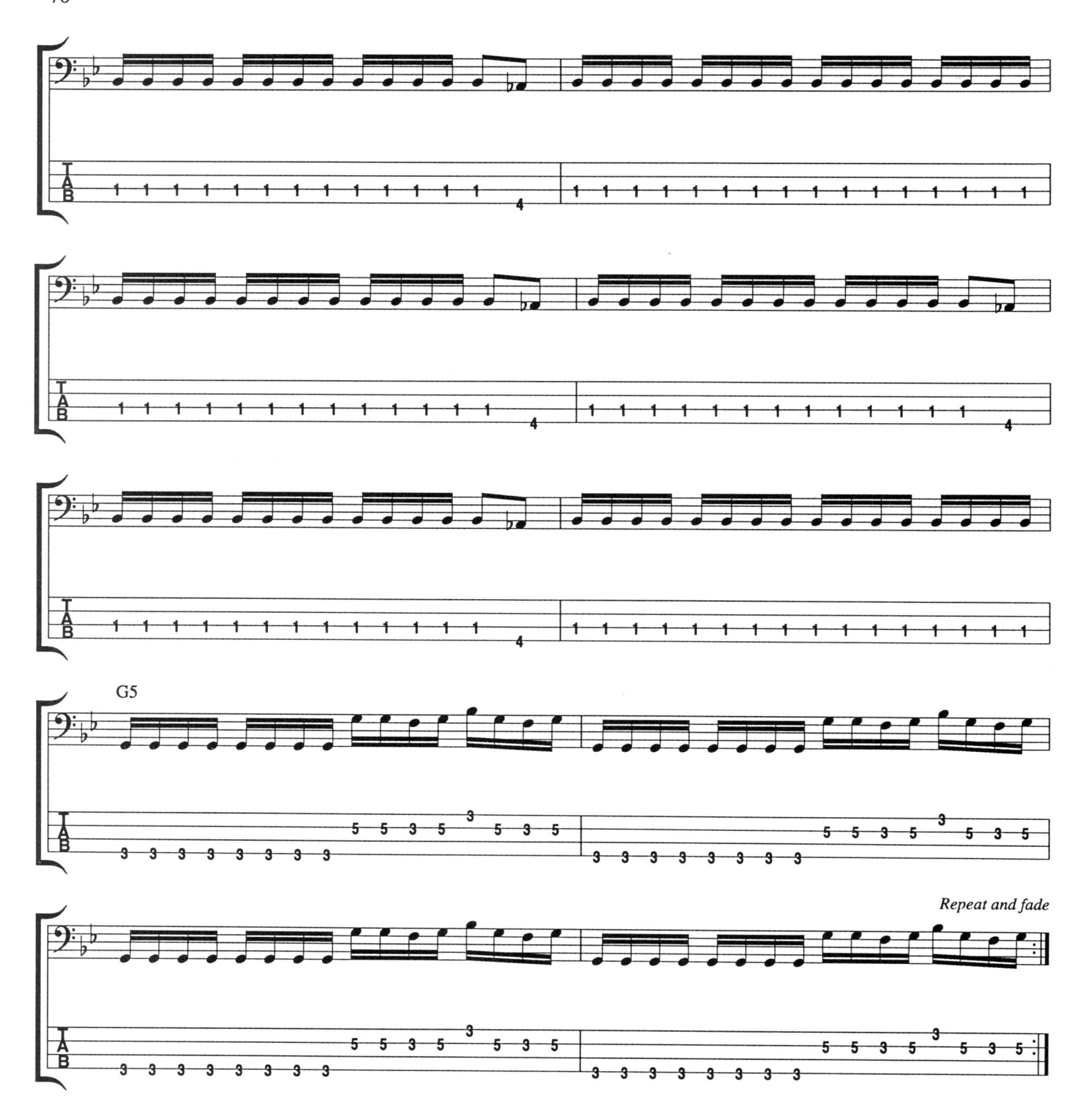

Verse 3:
I'm gonna keep on the run, I'm gonna have me some fun,
If it costs me my very last dime.
If I wind up broke then I always remember,
That I had a swingin' time.
I'm gonna give it everything I've got,
Lady Luck, please let the dice stay hot.
Let me shoot a seven with every shot.
(To Chorus:)

BASS GUITAR TAB GLOSSARY

TABLATURE EXPLANATION

TABLATURE is a four line staff that graphically represents the Bass fretboard. The numbers are the frets and the lines are the strings. The low E string is on the bottom and the G string is on the top.

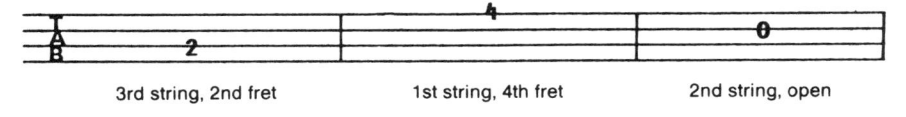

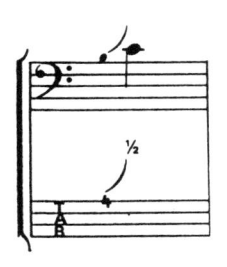

3rd string, 2nd fret   1st string, 4th fret   2nd string, open

BEND (half step): Play the note and bend up ½ step (one fret).

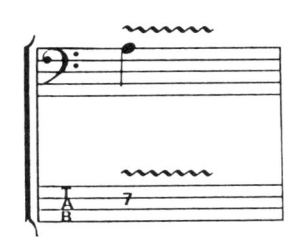

VIBRATO: The string is vibrated by shaking a held note with the fret hand. (Shake the finger, wrist, and forearm.)

SLIDE: Same as above except the second note is struck.

BEND (whole step): Play the note and bend up a whole step. (2 frets)

SLIDE: Strike the string from an unspecified pitch (usually one or two frets away) and slide into the note/fret.

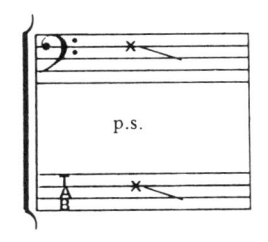

PICK SLIDE: (Nail Slide): The edge of the pick is slid down the edge of the string or string(s).

BEND and RELEASE: Play the note and gradually bend to the next pitch, then release to the original note.

SLIDE: Play the note and slide up an indefinite number of frets releasing the finger pressure near the end of the slide.

HAMMER ON: Play the lower note, then sound the higher note by hammering on with finger without picking it.

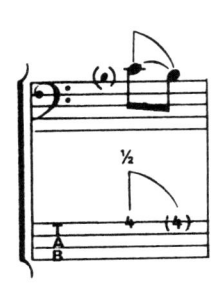

PREBEND and RELEASE: Bend the string, play it, then release to the original note.

SLIDE (Gliss): The first note is struck, then the same finger of the fret hand moves up or down the string to the location of the second note. The second note is not struck.

PULL OFF: Place both fingers on notes to be sounded. Play the higher note, then sound the lower note by pulling off the higher while keeping the lower note fretted.

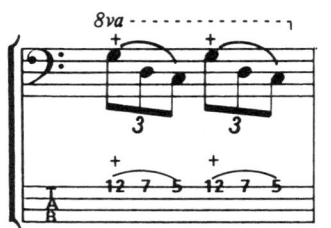

FRETBOARD TAPPING: Hammer on to the fretboard with the index or middle finger of the pick hand, then pull off to the note fretted by the fret hand.

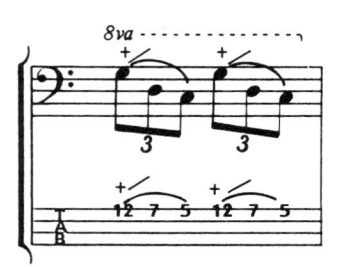

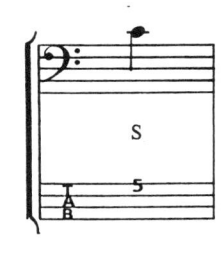

SNAP: Usually combined with the thumb technique, one of the fingers is plucked up to create a "snap." This is done on the higher strings and can alternate with the thumb.

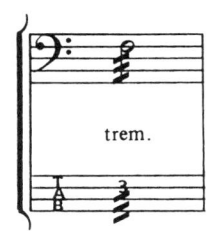

TRILL: The smaller notes (or numbers in parentheses) are hammered on and pulled off over and over for the length of the note.

TAP SLIDE and TAP PICK SLIDE: Same as Fretboard tapping but the finger or pick taps, slides up, then is pulled off to the fretted notes.

TREMOLO: The note is struck as rapidly and continuously as possible.

STACCATO (Short Notes): Notes should be played as short as possible. (Separated from one another)

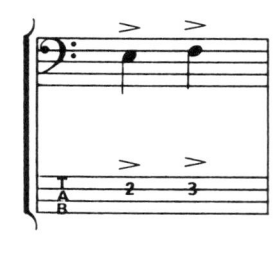

BEND AND TAP ON TECHNIQUE: Strike the note and bend up ½ or whole steps, then tap on the same string with pick hand fingertip at correct pitch or fret.

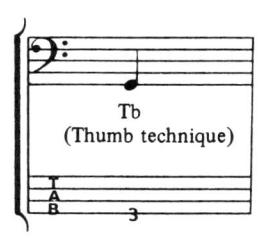

OPEN HARMONIC (Natural Harmonic): The fret hand lightly touches the string over the fret indicated; then it is struck. A chime sound is produced.

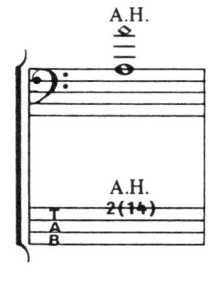

ACCENT: Note should be played with special emphasis creating an accent.

THUMB TECHNIQUE: Strike the string with the side of the outstretched thumb of the pick hand. (This is done with a wrist motion)

ARTIFICIAL HARMONIC: The fret hand frets the note indicated. The pick hand produces the harmonic by using a finger to lightly touch the string at the fret indicated in parentheses and plucking with another finger.

CHOPPY PHRASING: Notes should be accented with extreme staccato.

PALM MUTE: The note(s) is partially muted by the palm of the pick hand lightly touching the string(s) just before the bridge.